*Social Aspects
of Early Christianity*

social aspects of early christianity

Abraham J. Malherbe

Second Edition, Enlarged

FORTRESS PRESS   Philadelphia

Chapter Four, "Hospitality and Inhospitality in the Church," first appeared as "The Inhospitality of Diotrephes," in *God's Christ and His
People: Studies in Honour of Nils Alstrup Dahl,* edited by Jacob Jervell
and Wayne A. Meeks (Oslo: Universitetsforlaget, 1977) pp. 222–32
and is here reprinted by permission.

First published in 1977 by Louisiana State University Press
Second Edition, Enlarged by Fortress Press, 1983

Library of Congress Cataloging in Publication Data

Malherbe, Abraham J.
    Social aspects of early Christianity.

    Includes index.
    1. Sociology, Christian—History—Early church, ca.
30–600—Addresses, essays, lectures.   I. Title.
    BR166.M34 1983   270.1   83–5602
    ISBN 0–8006–1748–7

K121C83   Printed in the United States of America   1–1748

For Phyllis

Contents

Preface and
Acknowledgments

I HAVE attempted in this book to identify certain issues, problems, and prospects that might profitably engage the attention of scholars interested in sociological study of early Christianity. Personal interests, if not always competence, have naturally influenced selection of the topics, as well as the way in which they were approached. I can only hope that the approach has not been entirely idiosyncratic and that it will contribute to an enterprise that will occupy scholars of Christian antiquity for some time to come.

The substance of this book was delivered as the Rockwell Lectures at Rice University in April, 1975. It is a pleasure to express my thanks to Niels C. Nielsen, Jr., and his colleagues and to Henry M. Rockwell for their gracious hospitality. The lectures were prepared with an audience of nonspecialists in mind, and I have accordingly limited the scope and detail of the book. More technical discussion has been relegated to the notes, though it will be obvious to the *savant* that they are intended to be suggestive only.

Two matters need to be stated. First, *early Christianity*, as used herein, means Christianity as it is reflected in the New

Testament. Second, my admiration for the generation of scholars spanning the last decades of the nineteenth and the first decades of the twentieth centuries must be recorded. That the work of Adolf Deissmann, for example, receives as much attention as it does is not due to errors that he may have made, but to the greatness of his accomplishments, which require that we still take him seriously. *Sic itur ad astra*.

Preface to the
Second Edition

WHEN THESE lectures were delivered in 1975, sociological study of the New Testament was only beginning to be undertaken again with some seriousness. A new constituency has now emerged in the professional community which is pursuing the study with as much self-consciousness as vigor. The lectures were intended to provide information on the efforts that had been made and to suggest areas in which future work might profitably be done. Some of these areas, as well as many others, have received scholarly attention since then, and there is every indication that the field is rapidly gaining in popularity, a development that is not without its own problems. I am pleased that the book was still thought to be of sufficient interest to justify a second edition, and I am especially happy for the opportunity to add Chapter 4 and an Epilogue, along with a revised Index. My own work has been focused elsewhere and is only tangentially related to what is discussed in the book. Nevertheless, the reflections of an interested observer may not be completely without interest or value.

1
Prolegomena

NEW TESTAMENT scholarship is currently enjoying a great vitality, demonstrated less by the fervor with which its established disciplines are being pursued than by the criticism to which they are being subjected.[1] Those who question the accepted categories of New Testament scholarship wish to make it clear, however, that their restlessness is not a symptom of malaise but of the vigor and optimism with which they may reinvent their own disciplines.[2] The interest in early Christianity as a social phenomenon, with which this book is concerned, is an expression of that intention to move the study of early Christianity ahead.

Various reasons for the sociological interest may be suggested. For some scholars parochialism in dealing with Christian origins has become intolerable. Three generations ago

1. See, for example, James M. Robinson, "Introduction: The Dismantling and Reassembling of the Categories of New Testament Scholarship," in James M. Robinson and Helmut Koester, *Trajectories through Early Christianity* (Philadelphia, 1971), 1–19; Helmut Koester, "New Testament Introduction: A Critique of a Discipline," in Jacob Neusner (ed.), *Christianity, Judaism and Other Greco-Roman Cults: Studies for Morton Smith at Sixty* (4 vols.; Leiden, Holland, 1975), I, 1–20.

2. *Cf.*, Wayne A. Meeks, "The Social World of Early Christianity," *Bulletin of the Council on the Study of Religion*, VI (1975), 1.

students of Christian antiquity were usually the beneficiaries of a classical education which made them see Christianity as part of its cultural and social environments. In the decades since, the orientation has been more theological and literary. We have become content to repeat what Adolf Deissmann or Ernst von Dobschütz might have written around the turn of the century on the social circumstances of early Christianity, oblivious of the self-criticism implicit in our dependence on them. Students of Christian origins who wish to move beyond the treatments of an older generation have found themselves frustrated by the nature of the sources and their interpretation in the standard reference works on ancient society and religion.

Convinced of the need to give special attention to nonliterary and archaeological data, and to do so in collaboration with classicists, one group of scholars has focused on the religion and culture of the Aegean in early Christian times.[3] Their aims are to examine certain aspects of Greco-Roman society for whatever light might be thrown on early Christianity, to assemble collections of source materials that will serve further research, and to provide a new generation of scholars with the competence to continue research. Although the interests of this group are broader than sociological study, their work will perforce be concerned with aspects of ancient life that will aid such study.

Another reason for the sociological interest of those involved in this enterprise is their discontent with the present status of historical inquiry and theological interpretation. To many the hermeneutic discussions of a decade or two ago became increasingly esoteric and unappealing. As American biblical scholarship has become more independent and self-confident,

3. The project is under the leadership of Helmut Koester of Harvard University. Preliminary results of the first two years' activities have been communicated in a newsletter to be known as *Numina Aegaea*.

it has opened itself to new questions, frequently questions suggested by the emerging social sciences; and the axioms of previous generations have been subjected to close scrutiny. The development and growth in numbers of departments of religious studies in universities and colleges, many without religious affiliation, have contributed to this questioning.[4] In such settings the perspective from which early Christianity is studied is no longer that of the church.

In making a case for their enterprise, representatives of the sociological interest may at times consciously aim at fostering dissatisfaction with the predominance of theological and related concerns or point to "an overemphasis on a literary-historical and theological point of view to the detriment of the sociological."[5] This is not to say that the appropriateness of a theological perspective is denied—so long as it does not exclude the use of social-scientific disciplines. The leaders in this enterprise do not consider their work iconoclastic. In many ways. they see it as a natural outgrowth of what has been done in the

4. This does not imply that sociological interest in early Christianity is purely an American phenomenon. The work of E. A. Judge and Gerd Theissen, which will be discussed in this book, exhibits such interest in Australia and Germany, respectively; and the writings of Peter Brown, the British scholar, demonstrate, at least for a later period in the history of early Christianity, an established interest. What is significant on the American scene is the organization of activity within the American Academy of Religion (AAR) and the Society of Biblical Literature (SBL) to study the social world of early Christianity. Sociological interest in Christian origins should further be seen in the context of that approach to non-Christian religions both ancient and modern, where sociological interest is well established even if characterized by diversity. It could be argued that New Testament scholarship has been slower to engage in sociological treatment of its sources than has Old Testament scholarship. A useful orientation is provided by Jonathan Z. Smith, "The Social Description of Early Christianity," *Religious Studies Review*, I (1975), 19–21, prepared for the 1973 organizational meeting, sponsored by the AAR and SBL, of a group to study the social world of early Christianity. The decision was reached at that meeting to concentrate on Antioch and emphasize the "realia" upon which a social history may be based, maintaining an awareness of methodology and perspective. See Meeks, "Social World," 1.

5. John G. Gager, *Kingdom and Community: The Social World of Early Christianity* (Englewood Cliffs, N.J., 1975), 3.

3

traditional disciplines, but they perceive a need to be sensitive to new insights and issues if our understanding of early Christianity is materially to advance.

Interest in the sociological study of early Christianity is sufficiently strong to justify anticipation of a new constituency emerging within the professional community.[6] Thus, it is not surprising that doctoral dissertations are being written on subjects dealing with various social aspects of the early church.[7] Since young scholars are receiving their training in this atmosphere and are developing their research skills and perceptions in dealing with social questions, these formative influences may significantly direct the work that will occupy New Testament scholarship in the next generation.

I

The interest in early Christianity as a social phenomenon is not new. At the beginning of this century the subject was extensively discussed but, with few exceptions, was abandoned in the period between the two world wars. The major exceptions were Ernst Lohmeyer and the so-called Chicago School. Lohmeyer published in 1921 a useful little book that surveys the economic and social conditions of the Greco-Roman world and the early church.[8] For the most part it is a balanced presentation of the facts and a useful tool for attempting to place Christianity in its social context. In many ways it is a summary

6. *Ibid.*, 14.
7. For example, S. Scott Bartchy, *Mallon chresai: First Century Slavery and the Interpretation of I Corinthians 7:21*, Society of Biblical Literature Dissertation Series, XI (Missoula, Mont., 1973); Ronald F. Hock, "The Working Apostle: An Examination of Paul's Means of Livelihood" (Ph.D. Dissertation, Yale University, 1974); David L. Balch, "'Let Wives Be Submissive . . .': The Origin, Form and Apologetic Function of the Household Duty Code (Haustafel) in I Peter" (Ph.D. Dissertation, Yale University, 1974).
8. Ernst Lohmeyer, *Soziale Fragen im Urchristentum* (Darmstadt, Germany, 1973). See also Rudolf Schumacher, *Die soziale Lage der Christen im apostolischen Zeitalter* (Paderborn, Germany, 1924).

of the results of previous work, yet it has an independent viewpoint. The chief weakness of Lohmeyer's work, for our purpose, is that it is too general in nature. He sketches the phenomena that interest us; but rarely does he relate his discussion to the text of the New Testament. Furthermore, his book was written before the major contributions to our knowledge of the ancient world were made by scholars like Michael Rostovtzeff and, more recently and interestingly, Ramsay MacMullen. It is unfortunate that the kinds of questions that concerned Lohmeyer were not taken up by the standard introductions to the "background" of early Christianity represented by C. K. Barrett and by Johannes Leipoldt and Walter Grundmann.[9]

It is probably significant that the interest shown in social questions during this period between the world wars was by Americans, among whom the best known were Shirley Jackson Case and Shailer Mathews, both of Chicago. They were the major exponents of the sociohistorical approach that became the hallmark of the Chicago School and, in the minds of some Europeans, characteristic of American biblical scholarship. Americans who found their approach congenial denied that it was simply a survival of an exploded empiricism; they insisted that it represented "rather a conviction that all aspects of primitive Christianity, not only its external phenomena but the kerygmatic faith itself, are relative to social-cultural factors," and that no dichotomy could be made between faith and history.[10] It was argued that the American experience and char-

9. The attempts to provide sketches of New Testament *Zeitgeschichte* are generally too sweeping to more than occasionally touch on topics of sociological interest. See, for example, Werner Foerster, *Neutestamentliche Zeitgeschichte* (2 vols.; Hamburg, 1955–56), especially the English translation of Volume I by Gordon E. Harris under the title *From the Exile to Christ* (Philadelphia, 1964). Carl Schneider, *Geistesgeschichte des antiken Christentums* (2 vols.; Munich, 1954), is useful as an introduction to many subjects of interest.

10. Amos N. Wilder, "Biblical Hermeneutic and American Scholarship," in Walther Eltester (ed.), *Neutestamentliche Studien für Rudolf Bultmann zu seinem siebzigsten Geburtstag* (2nd ed.; Berlin, 1957), 25.

acter themselves contributed to making American scholars markedly interested in "the origin and history of Christianity as social movement and less so in the history of its ideas and doctrines."[11]

Shirley Jackson Case was the foremost figure of the Chicago School. Shunning metaphysical speculations, he insisted on a strictly functional approach that regarded the development of the early church's practices, theology, and ethics as responses to the needs of each generation. That such an approach was fully congenial to scholars identified with the social gospel is immediately obvious. Case studied particular persons, communities, and their circumstances because of his insistence that Christianity did not exist apart from them. But, as Leander Keck has pointed out, he "did not really analyze sociologically the groups and communities which composed early Christianity, but, relying on his functional view of religion, was apparently content to generalize on the basis of ideas and social aspects of the Greco-Roman world."[12] What Case did not accomplish, namely the concrete and detailed delineation of the social world and style of life of the early Christian communities, is what Keck calls for.

In view of the current interest in the sociology of knowledge, Keck regards the work of Shailer Mathews as possibly more suggestive today than that of Case. "Mathews was interested in the way the social mind affected theology. By 'social mind' he meant 'a more or less general community of conscious states, processes, ideas, interests, and ambitions which to a greater or less degree repeats itself in the experience of individuals belonging to the group characterized by this community of consciousness.' For him, 'doctrine is the result of a dominant so-

11. *Ibid.*, 30.
12. Leander E. Keck, "On the Ethos of Early Christians," *Journal of the American Academy of Religion*, XLII (1974), 437.

cial mind at work in religion.'" [13] Despite the shortcomings of the work of Case and Mathews, Keck feels that they do alert us to weaknesses he perceives in recent work in the New Testament, particularly in the efforts to write a New Testament theology. Rudolf Bultmann, for example, is criticized because he did not relate the theologies of Paul and John very clearly to the communities for which they wrote, with the result that "one has the impression that their theologies were not really affected by the hurly-burly of early Christian life." [14]

Keck's discussions of the works of Ernst von Dobschütz and Herbert Preisker demonstrate that the current interest in social description should not necessarily be described as antitheological. Rather, Keck perceives inadequacies in the way that the theological enterprise has been conducted and insists that an awareness of the sociohistorical context is necessary for a satisfactory understanding of the documents that form the basis for any attempt at theological reconstruction. This insistence does not betray a desire to reject historical and literary criticism or the gains that they have made. But it does demand that the documents and the traditions behind them be related to their *Sitze im Leben* as that term was originally understood by Hermann Gunkel—a sociological category, not simply a description of historical context. The stress is therefore on studying Christian communities in particular places; it is hoped that this would prepare the way for ascertaining how traditions functioned in those communities. [15]

The neglect of early Christianity's social context and social make-up during the last sixty years is surprising in light of the intensity with which the subject was discussed around the turn of the century. The efforts of certain members of the so-

13. *Ibid.*, 438.
14. *Ibid.*, 439.
15. *Ibid.*, 446ff.

called *religionsgeschichtliche Schule* during the last decades of the nineteenth century related the organization of the early Christian congregations to those of other conventicles and sects in the Roman Empire, especially the various kinds of guilds and philosophical schools.[16] That examination of the latter may bear fruit for our understanding of early Christian groups has recently been demonstrated[17] and will occupy our attention later in this chapter.

Socialist historians early in this century also were dealing with Christianity and its social environment. Strictly speaking, their interest was sociological rather than historical. For them "it is society which produces both personality and documents, and since each successive generation and sect of Christianity has managed to create a Founder in its own image and likeness, we are to assume that the first generation did no better."[18] Karl Kautsky, the Marxist historian of socialism, serves as an illustration of this approach. He saw the first generation of Christians as proletarian in character. Uneducated, oppressed, and far removed from the masses of the people, their doctrine and the history of their communities were confined to oral traditions that could not be tested by outsiders. Those traditions were put into writings as more educated people became Christians; therefore they are not to be taken as reliable sources to describe the origin of Christianity, but they can give us an idea of the movement itself. That movement was proletarian and was prompted by economic and social distress. It "is of no sig-

16. For an account of the discussion, see Olof Linton, *Das Problem der Urkirche in den neueren Forschung* (Uppsala, Sweden, 1932), esp. 31ff.; for further treatment of this subject, see pp. 24–28, 87–90 herein.

17. Robert L. Wilken, "Collegia, Philosophical Schools, and Theology," in Stephen Benko and John J. O'Rourke (eds.), *The Catacombs and the Colosseum: The Roman Empire as the Setting of Primitive Christianity* (Valley Forge, Pa., 1971), 268–91.

18. James Shiel, *Greek Thought and the Rise of Christianity* (New York, 1968), 91.

nificance for our historical insight to be instructed as to the personality of Jesus and his disciples," but "it is of the utmost importance to be clear about the character of the Christian community." [19] The first Christian community in Jerusalem gave expression to its proletarian character and what appears to have been the social gospel of Jesus in the communism it practiced in its early years. This communism was abandoned as Christianity became more conservative, attracting people from the administrative classes of the Empire. Whereas it had begun as a revolutionary movement against the rulers, it now began to develop in a new way under the influence of its own ruling class, in which the office of bishop was the most significant feature. [20] For Kautsky, then, ideology yielded to economics, and the social factors were more important than persons.

In response to such a socialist interpretation of early Christianity, Ernst Troeltsch argued that neither Jesus nor the early church was concerned with social reform. Christianity did appeal to the lower classes, which formed communities on a genuine religious basis. Jesus himself had been a man of the people, but his expectation of the kingdom of God made social and economic aspirations irrelevant. His followers were able to form religious communities on the basis of their faith in a divine revelation. "The meaning and capacity for development of the religious movement which arose in this way were always dependent on the power and depth of the stimulus which had been imported by such a naive revelation, and, on the other hand, upon the energy of the religious conviction which gave to this stimulus a divine and absolute authority." [21] However, that the earliest church was opposed to social and civic cus-

19. Karl Kautsky, *The Foundations of Christianity*, trans. H. F. Mins (New York, 1953), 274f.

20. *Ibid.*, 364, 380f., 448.

21. Ernst Troeltsch, *The Social Teaching of the Christian Churches*, trans. Olive Wyon (2 vols.; 1931; New York, 1960), I, 44.

toms did not mean for Troeltsch that it was unaffected by the social situation.

The religious community has to do something for its members beyond the mere preaching of salvation; it has to provide men with shelter and assistance during the period of their earthly struggle. Thus the influence of the social situation becomes direct as soon as the Christian community is able to give help on those lines. But the more the Christian community becomes a society within a society, a state within a State, the more strongly it becomes conscious of the fact that it is bound up with concrete social problems, and it then turns its attention and its power of organization to these matters. All this, however, is simply the result of the new religious idea; it is not its starting-point.[22]

How New Testament scholars reacted to the socialist interpretation represented by Kautsky can be illustrated by the work of von Dobschütz. He was convinced that historical progress could not be explained by forces originating in a collective way but by eminent leaders or heroes. "The astonishing success of the Gospel during the first century is the work of St. Paul and his fellow-labourers, not of the mass of Christian converts whom they brought together by their preaching. The character of the simple communities owes much more to the founder than to the former situation of the individual members."[23] He seeks to demonstrate that it is a new spirit, the Holy Spirit introduced by Christianity, which created moral judgment and strength and manifested itself with power in communities. The Holy Spirit made Christians of heathen and Jews, and had "trained the immature into an intelligent and

22. Ibid., 50. For a rejection of Troeltsch's viewpoint, see Gager, Kingdom and Community, 131.
23. Ernst von Dobschütz, Christian Life in the Primitive Church, trans. George Bremner and W. D. Morrison (New York, 1904), xv. See also Adolf Deissmann's review of Kautsky in Light from the Ancient East, trans. Lionel R. M. Strachan (4th ed.; Grand Rapids, Mich., 1965), 465–67.

fully conscious Christianity." [24] Keck expresses his appreciation for much of von Dobschütz's work, especially his positive attitude toward the development of institutional stabilization in the third and fourth generations of the church. But he calls into question von Dobschütz's assessment of the importance of the founders of communities for the character of those communities. [25] Keck sees the creative forces to be located more in the communities than in their leaders.

II

The sociological approach to early Christianity is to be welcomed as one method among others that we may utilize. That a clearer view of Christian communities will help us to understand both early Christianity and its literature better is surely beyond doubt. But we should beware of excessive enthusiasm. For example, although it is not at all clear that Paul and his coworkers were primarily responsible for the growth of the church in the first century, it is not immediately obvious that the communities apart from their leaders will provide us with the information we seek about early Christianity. The communities themselves came into existence in response to preaching, and social factors no doubt contributed to that response. But it was to the preaching that appeal was made in the documents that sought to direct the life and thought of the communities. [26] The social character of the communities does appear, in some cases, to have contributed to the conditions that called forth the documents and does enable us to grasp more firmly the intention of those documents. It is therefore of the utmost

24. von Dobschütz, *Christian Life*, xxviii–xxix.
25. Keck, "On the Ethos of Early Christians," 441–43. See also Gager, *Kingdom and Community*, 66ff.
26. See, for example, Paul's references to the first principles of his preaching and teaching when he addresses himself to problems in Corinth: I Cor. 8:4–6; 11:23–26; 12:1–3; 15:3–5.

importance that we know as much as we can about them in order to understand the issues under discussion. The degree to which the initial preaching continued to influence the communities may have changed, especially as social forces acted upon them. In addition, the implications of the preaching may not have been perceived either by the founders or the communities they established. But those communities cannot be studied apart from the impulses that brought them into existence or from their relationship to their leaders.

It is natural in the study of social history to concentrate on communities, or readers, to whom extant documents were addressed, rather than on the writers.[27] However, given the importance ancient communities attached to their founders, the question of how a community understood itself can often only be established by examining its relationship to its founder or leader as well as the philosophical or theological teaching it received from him.[28] To accept too easily as a working hypothesis Kautsky's view that social factors were more important than persons, or to diminish the theological aspects of the communities' self-understanding, seems unwarranted.[29] But equally suspect is the contrary assertion—that the true historian should devote his attention to those outstanding few indi-

27. See E. A. Judge, *The Social Pattern of Christian Groups in the First Century* (London, 1960), 9f.

28. For the situation in Corinth, see James M. Robinson, "Kerygma and History in the New Testament," in Robinson and Koester, *Trajectories*, 30ff. Robinson points to the special relationship communities assumed to exist between themselves and their founders through their having been baptized by the founders (p. 32 *n.* 12), and he suggests that the Corinthians' heretical interpretation of the Pauline kerygma was behind the excesses that concern Paul in I Corinthians (p. 34).

29. See Gager, *Kingdom and Community*, 28ff., for a sympathetic treatment of the view that a prophet may be more important to a cult as a symbolic focus than as a source of authority and initiative. On the importance of social factors for religious leaders of various types, see Gerd Theissen, "Legitimation und Lebensunterhalt: Eine Beitrag zur Soziologie urchristlicher Missionäre," *New Testament Studies*, XXI (1975), 192–221.

viduals who by their own personal gifts of intellect and spirit mold the majority and move history ahead.[30] A more balanced approach might be to recognize the importance of the communal aspect of early Christianity while retaining an openness to the possible continuing importance of the churches' founders and leaders and what was conceived to be their theology.

Furthermore, we must be aware of the different relationships that were possible between the literature and the communities to which it was addressed. We must, for instance, resist the temptation to see so much of early Christian literature either as a community product or as reflecting the actual circumstances of the communities with which the writings are associated. We too frequently read of communities that virtually produced one or another of the Gospels or for which they were produced.[31] It is at least possible that some documents were rescued from obscurity, not because they represented the viewpoints of communities, but precisely because they challenged them. It is too facile to view literature as the product of communities. The relationships could have been very complex.

Groups that did not constitute organized communities are known to have produced bodies of literature reflecting their concerns. An example of this is the Cynic letters from the early Empire. Not real letters, these fictitious documents, purportedly written by the ancient heroes of the sect, are propaganda pieces; they are of major importance because they tell us what was considered important by the Cynics themselves and alert

30. Olof Gigon, *Die antike Kultur und das Christentum* (Darmstadt, Germany, 1967), 7. See also von Dobschütz, *Christian Life*, xv.
31. *Cf.*, Gager, *Kingdom and Community*, 8f., "The various images of Jesus whatever their relation to the historical Jesus of Nazareth, are in the first instance reflections of the communities that preserved and transmitted the Gospel traditions. . . . Thus the Gospels and their sources are models *of* as well as models *for* their respective groups."

us to the diversity of views they held.[32] But to what degree Cynics can be said to have constituted communities depends on how one defines *community*. It is unlikely that the highly individualistic Cynics had organized communities. They showed a certain community of interests, which is reflected in their writings; but this did not lead to the formation of social communities. That they are sometimes thought to have constituted a school or to have had organized conventicles demonstrates how easy it is to import something foreign when working by analogy.[33] The Cynics make us sensitive to the need for controls in establishing the relationship between literature and communities.

When such controls are used, we can see more clearly the character of the producers of a particular body of literature and also see that the situation may have been reversed: the literature may have produced the group. Some scholars have argued that this was the case with Roman Pythagoreanism. One school of thought denies that there was any continuity between classical and Roman Pythagoreanism. In the Hellenistic age there appeared a Pythagorean literature, vexingly difficult to date with any certainty; yet there is no evidence that points to the existence of a group with Pythagorean beliefs during that period. It is that literature, however, which is thought to have

32. On these letters, see especially Eduard Norden, "Beiträge zur Geschichte der griechischen Philosophie," *Jahrbuch für classische Philologie*, Supplementary Vol. XIX (1893), 393; Kurt von Fritz, "Quellenuntersuchungen zu Leben und Philosophie des Diogenes von Sinope," *Philologus*, Supplementary Vol. XVIII, Pt. 2 (1926), pp. 63–71; Victor E. Emeljanow, "The Letters of Diogenes" (Ph.D. Dissertation, Stanford University, 1968).

33. *Cf.*, Samuel Dill, *Roman Society from Nero to Marcus Aurelius* (New York, 1956), 351; Rudolf Helm, "Kynismus," Pauly-Wissowa, *Realenzyklopädie*, XII (1924), 12. On the proper use of analogy in research in comparative religion, see Gerhard Kittel, *Die Religionsgeschichte und das Urchristentum* (Gütersloh, Germany, 1932), 9. On the problems associated with using analogy in historical study, see William F. Albright, *Archaeology, Historical Analogy, and Early Biblical Tradition* (Baton Rouge, 1966), esp. Chap. 1. On a distinction between genealogical and analogical parallels, see Deissmann, *Light from the Ancient East*, 265ff.

called into existence the Pythagoreans of the Roman period.[34] This is not to suggest, of course, that the earliest Christian literature available to us was a blueprint for the establishment of the communities we wish to understand. It is only to illustrate the various relationships that may exist between groups and their literature.

These comments of concern express the conviction that our major sources for the social reconstruction of early Christianity are literary. We may expect to gain insights elsewhere—for example, from archaeological data and modern social theory; but eventually we are driven back to literary sources. With that in mind we must stress the obvious, namely that sociological study of early Christianity cannot slight literary criticism. We must persist in seeking to determine the character and intention of different types of literature if we hope to discern how they functioned in relation to the communities with which they were associated. When that is done they can more properly be assessed as witnesses to particular communities.

Church orders, for example, tend to present their instructions as though they were traditional and universal practice, grounding their legitimacy in that ostensible fact. They are therefore less valuable as sources for information about actual practices and situations in particular communities than are letters, which tend to stress specifics.[35] Letters, according to ancient epistolary theory, are substitutes for their writers'

---

34. This is the view of Walter Burkert, "Hellenistische Pseudopythagorica," *Philologus*, CV (1961), 16–43, 226–46. He takes into account both literary and archaeological (Porta Maggiore) evidence. This reading of the evidence stresses the respectful view of Pythagoras as the patron saint of philosophy. *Cf.*, A. D. Nock, "Sarcophagi and Symbolism," *American Journal of Archaeology*, L (1946), 153f., most readily accessible in Zeph Stewart (ed.), *Essays on Religion and the Ancient World* (2 vols.; Cambridge, Mass., 1972), II, 622f. See also Ramsay MacMullen, *Enemies of the Roman Order: Treason, Unrest and Alienation in the Empire* (Cambridge, Mass., 1966), Chap. 3.

35. *Cf.*, Wilhelm Schmid and Otto Stählin, *Geschichte der griechischen Literatur* (8 vols.; Munich, 1924), Vol. II, Pt. 2, pp. 1234f.

presence[36] and thus add another dimension to the social situation: In addition to providing us with information important to the writers and possibly to the recipients, they also say something about a community's relationship to someone outside it. In its intention and character, an apology is different from a letter or even from polemic. A primary feature of apologetic, properly understood, is that it offers an exposition of the beliefs and life of the challenged community. But what it gives an exposition of is not so much determined by the community's own set of priorities as by the challenges it addresses itself to. The very form in which the apology is made may be determined by the particular nature of the charge.[37] It would be rash, therefore, to reconstruct communities from apologies without the aid of other evidence enabling us clearly to perceive the function of the apology in its sociological context. What is called for is greater appreciation of the sociological functions of the different types of literature with which we are concerned.[38]

Assuming the legitimacy of the enterprise as well as an awareness of the dangers of hastiness in adopting certain approaches, where do we begin a social reconstruction of early

36. For example, see the Weichert editions of ps. Demetrius *Typoi Epistolikoi*, p. 2, ll. 19ff., on the "friendly" letter, and ps. Proclus *Peri Epistolimaiou Characteros*, p. 27, l. 10, as well as the discussions in Heikki Koskenniemi, *Studien zur Idee und Phraseologie des griechischen Briefes bis 400 n. Chr.* (Helsinki, 1956), 38ff., and Klaus Thraede, *Grundzüge griechisch-römischer Brieftopik* (Munich, 1970), 25ff. For the relevance of the theory to Paul's letters, see Robert W. Funk, "The Apostolic Parousia: Form and Function," in William R. Farmer, C. F. D. Moule, and Richard R. Niebuhr (eds.), *Christian History and Interpretation: Studies Presented to John Knox* (Cambridge, 1967), 249–68.

37. On the purpose of Christian apologetic literature, see Jean Danielou, *Gospel Message and Hellenistic Culture*, trans. John A. Baker (London, 1973), 7–37, and the literature cited there. On the literary forms of apologetic, see Hermann Jordan, *Geschichte der altchristlichen Literatur* (Leipzig, Germany, 1911), 211ff., and Abraham J. Malherbe, "The Structure of Athenagoras, 'Supplicatio pro Christianis,'" *Vigiliae Christianae*, XXIII (1969), 1ff.

38. See Donald W. Riddle, *The Martyrs: A Study in Social Control* (Chicago, 1931), esp. 99–122.

Christianity? Keck suggests that one might proceed by writ-ing the history of Christianity in particular places, working by analogy—studying non-Christian communities, analyzing Christian communities as they had evolved in the second cen-tury, observing them in light of what we know of the behavior of minority groups, and bringing to bear the sociology of knowl-edge.[39] But a prior consideration must be an assessment of the sources available for the enterprise. The sources that concern us are, primarily, the New Testament writings, and then other early Christian writings. We must begin with these writings, and we must read them with a sensitivity to their social dimen-sions before we hasten to draw larger patterns.

Most of the New Testament writings are letters, occasional in nature, that provide us with information about the recipients and their communities, and sometimes the writers. They are concerned with the communities rather than with society as a whole, and they enable us to learn of their problems and aspi-rations. The value of the New Testament writings lies in their particularity—they deal with concrete situations. "The New Testament is not an orderly statement of dogma, but a het-erogeneous collection of writings addressed to various occa-sions."[40] It is axiomatic in modern scholarship that they should be understood in relation to those situations. Any seri-ous attempt at homogenization will lead to imprecision or even error. For that reason the principle of analogy should be used with the greatest caution.

To say that we must begin with the New Testament is to be aware of the myopia with which the task may consequently be carried out. We must recognize the problems inherent in be-ginning at the other end, that is, with the nonbiblical literary material. Compared with that material, the New Testament

39. Keck, "On the Ethos of Early Christians," 449.
40. Judge, *Social Pattern of Christian Groups*, 9.

writings do not appear to be poor evidence at all. E. A. Judge, the Australian ancient historian, has recently argued that the New Testament offers a focal point around which Greek society of the Julio-Claudian era as well as diaspora Judaism can be reconstructed, for in his view the New Testament contributes one of our most coherent sets of documents for both. He admits that one might start from either side of the fence but cautions that "those who work out from the New Testament quickly find themselves off solid ground due to the poor control we have over the strictly contemporary material."[41] He offers examples of how the work of ancient historians, utilizing literary and epigraphic data, might improve the situation, since they see the New Testament as a focal point for their own studies. Judge's work is important, as is that of Ramsay MacMullen, the Yale ancient historian, who in masterly fashion mines material of diverse character to weave together a picture of various social aspects of the Roman Empire. It is not, then, without appreciation for the value of nonliterary sources that I desire to give closer attention to the problem of our literary sources. My concern witnesses to the limitations of my own competence as well as my desire to discover what literary sources outside the New Testament are the most appropriate ones for us to examine.

The level of literary culture displayed by the New Testament will occupy us at greater length in the second chapter. Suffice it here to say that, with some exceptions, the New Testament writings are what the Germans call *Volksliteratur*

---

41. E. A. Judge, "St. Paul and Classical Society," *Jahrbuch für Antike und Christentum*, XV (1972), 25. See also Judge's "The Early Christians as a Scholastic Community," *Journal of Religious History*, I (1960–61), 7; Adolf von Harnack, *Die Mission und Ausbreitung des Christentums in den ersten drei Jahrhunderten* (4th ed.; Leipzig, Germany, 1924), preface. Von Harnack claims that we know more about the early church than we know about all the oriental religions that established themselves in the Roman Empire before Constantine.

or *Kleinliteratur*, writings designed for mass consumption. They represent the literary forms congenial to the masses and speak of the peoples' concerns. [42] But most of the pagan literature preserved from the period comes instead from literary or philosophical sophisticates. On the surface, therefore, it may appear that the literature will only be of limited value in our attempts to situate early Christianity in its social context. However, just as the New Testament will yield upon close scrutiny information of sociological interest, so will the literature from the early Empire. [43] If we broaden our definition of literature sufficiently, we may include the papyri, which contain a wealth of information dealing with the lives of common people. This is well known, but the resource has not been significantly tapped by those interested in the social character of early Christianity. Moving upward on the literary and social scale are the various kinds of materials dealing with the Cynics, those philosophical street preachers who sought the moral reformation of the masses. Much is still to be learned from this source. Related to the Cynics, but higher on the scale, are men like Dio Chrysostom, who also traveled as physicians of men's souls but comported themselves with greater dignity and refinement. Dio's discourses are important sources for conditions in major cities of the Empire around the turn of the first century, and

42. See Richard Reitzenstein, "Ein Stück hellenistischer Kleinliteratur," *Göttingische Gelehrte Anzeigen* (1904), 308ff.; Deissmann, *Light from the Ancient East*, 247ff.; Jordan, *Geschichte*, 64ff.
43. *Cf.*, Ramsay MacMullen's frustration in attempting to describe matters that were taken for granted or were regarded as undignified and therefore not mentioned in works of "literature," and in his inability to let peasants speak for themselves because of the paucity of firsthand literary sources, *Roman Social Relations: 50 B.C. to A.D. 284* (New Haven, Conn., 1974), 26, 28, 41. See also his "Peasants during the Principate," in Hildegard Temporini (ed.), *Aufstieg und Niedergang der römischen Welt* (7 vols. to date; Berlin, 1974—), Vol. II, Pt. 1, pp. 253–61. But, as MacMullen's own work shows, the task is not impossible. Since early Christianity was largely an urban phenomenon, and ancient writers represented an urban culture, our task is not as difficult.

they also provide a charming picture of peasant life.[44] Then there are the satirists, those critics who commented on the foibles of their fellowmen, thereby enabling us to catch glimpses of ancient society and to learn the views of the common people. It is thus understandable that such modern descriptions of Roman society as those by Ludwig Friedländer and Jerome Carcopino or Samuel Dill have frequent references to Horace, Juvenal, and Lucian.[45] The literary evidence must always be treated judiciously, with special attention to the biases of the writers, but this evidence can be used most effectively.

III

Sociological description of early Christianity can concentrate either on social facts or on sociological theory as a means of describing the 'sacred cosmos' or 'symbolic universe' of early Christian communities. Even though new historical information may be assimilated within old paradigms, we should strive to know as much as possible about the actual social circumstances of those communities before venturing theoretical descriptions or explanations of them.[46] With that conviction in mind I will illustrate some of the issues raised in this chapter by briefly examining the relationship between Paul's Thessalonian church and society.

The relationship between church and state is the most frequently treated of all the subjects that might engage us, because of the comparatively tangible character of political events. But that is not the prime concern of the New Testament writers, nor is it my concern here. The New Testament

44. See, for example, Eugen Wilmes, *Beiträge zur Alexandrinerrede or. 32 des Dion Chrysostomos* (Bonn, 1970), and Dio Chrysostom *Oration 7*.
45. On Juvenal, see Herold Weiss, "The *Pagani* among the Contemporaries of the First Christians," *Journal of Biblical Literature*, LXXXVI (1967), 42–52.
46. Gager, *Kingdom and Community*, 2–15, elects the other option. Judge, "St. Paul and Classical Society," has identified some of the major *desiderata* and suggested possible directions for research. Although he is primarily concerned with Paul, his comments have wider relevance.

writers respond more to social criticism than to questions about the legality of the Christians' status or actions. Given the tension that did exist between Christians and their larger society, the explicit comments made in the New Testament about non-Christians are remarkably free from condemnation.[47] In Paul's words, "What have I to do with judging outsiders? Is it not those inside the church whom you are to judge? God judges those outside" (I Cor. 5:12f.). Christians remain in a society that may be hostile to them, but they are not to retaliate in kind. The injunction from the Sermon on the Mount that Christians love their enemies is one of the New Testament passages most frequently used by the Church Fathers.[48] There are two kinds of sources for outsiders' views of Christians. The least ambiguous are explicit comments made by pagans about Christians.[49] Unfortunately, these begin only in the second century. The others are the New Testament writings themselves. They attribute actions or insults to pagans, though not extensively.[50] These writings also inculcate certain kinds of conduct designed to counter an opinion that outsiders might have of Christians. We can draw an informed generalization from all of these sources: In the first century Christians were criticized for social rather than political reasons. In the second century, as Christianity assumed a sepa-

47. See W. C. van Unnik, "Die Rücksicht auf die Reaktion der Nicht-Christen als Motiv in der altchristlichen Paränese," in Walther Eltester (ed.), *Judentum, Urchristentum, Kirche: Festschrift für Joachim Jeremias* (Berlin, 1964), 221–33.
48. See the index to Matthew 5:43–48 in Edouard Massaux, *Influence de l'Evangile de saint Matthieu sur la littérature chretienne avant saint Irénée* (Louvain, Belgium, 1950).
49. See Pierre de Labriolle, *La réaction paienne: Étude sur la polemique antichrétienne du Ier au VIe siècle* (Paris, 1934; repr. 1948); Wolfgang Speyer, "Zu den Vorwürfen der Heiden gegen die Christen," *Jahrbuch für Antike und Christentum*, VI (1963), 129–35; Milton V. Anastos, "Porphyry's Attack on the Bible," in L. Wallach (ed.), *The Classical Tradition: Literary and Historical Studies in Honor of Harry Caplan* (Ithaca, N.Y., 1966), 421–50, esp. the bibliography in notes 1 and 2; Léon Herrmann, *Chrestos: Temoignages paiens et juifs sur le christianisme du première siècle* (Brussels, 1970).
50. See pp. 52–53 herein.

21

rate identity in the Roman mind and became more politically significant, political action was directed against it. Christians tended to be lumped together with other exotic cults such as the Jews and the devotees of Isis, and with the unpopular Epicurean philosophical sect.

It could be expected that Christians, aware of the outsiders' views, would want to assert their distinctiveness and would do so in terms which would convey that distinctiveness to outsiders. In the second century they did so in apologetic writings that were ostensibly, at least, written for non-Christians. In these they often expressed a claim to be a third race, distinct from both the Jews and the Gentiles.[51] In the New Testament, however, the response to outside criticism is not directed to non-Christians but to the church. In the final analysis the behavior of Christians and the quality of their lives would be their unique response to society.[52] The specific ways in which that distinctiveness was practiced gives us an insight into how Christians may have been viewed by outsiders.

Paul wrote I Thessalonians to one of the first churches that he had established in Greece. Paul had spent, at most, only a few months with the church, which was largely made up of people converted from paganism. Having just been encouraged by Timothy, with respect to the Thessalonians' faith, Paul writes the letter to his recent converts to supply what is lacking in their faith—that is, to instruct them in certain practical aspects of the Christian life (Chap. 3). The last two chapters of the letter are clearly paraenetic, consisting of general moral exhortation. The first three chapters, however, are more prob-

---

51. See Adolf von Harnack, *The Mission and Expansion of Christianity in the First Three Centuries*, trans. and ed. James Moffatt (2 vols.; 1908; New York, 1961), I, 242–65. See also Abraham J. Malherbe, "The Apologetic Theology of the *Preaching of Peter*," *Restoration Quarterly*, XIII (1970), 205–23.

52. See Peter Lippert, *Leben als Zeugnis: Die werbende Kraft christlicher Lebensführung nach dem Kirchenverständnis neutestamentlicher Briefe* (Stuttgart, 1968).

lematic. In them, Paul uses two styles of discourse—the paraenetic style of exhortation, commonly employed by moral philosophers in the first century, and the antithetic style, which serves a paraenetic function and was used by these philosophers when introducing themselves to audiences that had invited them to speak.

These first three chapters are autobiographical, but the function of the autobiographical elements has been disputed. Using the antithetic style, Paul claims that his motivation to preach was not error or uncleanness; nor did he preach out of guile. Rather, he chose to preach so that he might please God (I Thess. 2:1–4). This kind of statement has led scholars to assume that Paul is denying charges that had been made against him. If he is, the autobiographical section of the letter would have an apologetic function, representing the major purpose of the entire letter; thus the last two chapters would tell us little about the church in Thessalonica.

The first three chapters, however, are paraenetic in function rather than apologetic. They not only enable us to learn more about the Thessalonian church and Paul's relationship with it, but, through the self-description, they also establish the basis for the exhortation in chapters four and five. The antithetic style is not apologetic and is entirely appropriate in this type of writing.[53] Paul also describes himself in terms used to describe philosophers who saw their aim to be the healing of men's souls: "For you remember our labor and toil, brethren; we worked night and day, that we might not burden any of you, while we preached to you the gospel of God" (I Thess. 2:9).

The style of paraenetic discourse, as it is used by Paul, stresses that what is being said is not new but a reminder of what the readers already know (e.g., I Thess. 1:5; 2:1f, 5, 9f; 3:3). It encourages them to continue doing what they are al-

53. Cf., Abraham J. Malherbe, "'Gentle as a Nurse': The Cynic Background to I Thess. ii," Novum Testamentum, XII (1970), 203–17.

ready doing (*e.g.*, 4:1, 9f; 5:11) and to imitate notable examples or models of the actions that are being urged (*cf.*, 1:6, 2:14). It also stresses the warm personal relationship between the writer and the readers.[54] The absence of any sign of tension between Paul and his recent converts is noteworthy. In fact, Paul goes beyond the normal paraenetic style in not merely calling them to imitate him, but claiming that they have already done so (1:6).

Since Paul's style in this letter is so heavily indebted to the popular philosophers, his statements of his self-support may also be clarified by examining what the philosophers had to say about their means of livelihood. It has recently been shown that Paul's custom of working to support himself was not a vestige of his former life as a Jewish rabbi. His practice and his comments on it are significant in the context of the popular philosophers' discussions of appropriate sources for their livelihood.[55] For example, Musonius Rufus in the first century saw value in the philosopher's working with his hands so that his pupils would benefit "by seeing him at work in the fields demonstrating by his own labour the lesson which philosophy inculcates—that one should endure hardships, and suffer the pains of labor with his own body, rather than depend on another for sustenance."[56] This view of a Stoic with Cynic leanings expresses an ideal that was not commonly realized by Stoic philosophers. In contrast, Paul confidently presents himself as a model who demonstrates the ideal.

The debate is further illustrated by Philodemus the Epicu-

54. For the understanding of I Thessalonians as a paraenetic letter, see Abraham J. Malherbe, "Hellenistic Moralists and the New Testament," in Hildegard Temporini (ed.), *Aufstieg und Niedergang der römischen Welt* (7 vols. to date; Berlin, 1976—), Vol. II, Pt. 3, where I Thessalonians 4:9–12 is also discussed at greater length.
55. See Hock, "The Working Apostle."
56. Musonius Rufus *Fragment* XI (p. 60, ll. 9–15) in the Hense edition; the translation quoted is that of Cora E. Lutz, *Musonius Rufus: The Roman Socrates*, Yale Classical Studies, X (New Haven, Conn., 1947), 83.

rean, who viewed the lot of the farmer who worked with his hands as miserable. He believed it was preferable to live off others' manual labor, "for then one is least entangled in business, the source of so many annoyances; there indeed is found a becoming way of life, a withdrawal into leisure with one's friends, and, for those who moderate their desires, the most honorable source of revenue."[57] For the Epicureans, who formed communities, withdrawal and quietism (*hesychia*) were of the utmost importance in attaining their goal, that calm blessedness (*ataraxia*) which could be attained only in company with others who were like-minded.[58] They took no part in public affairs and were not concerned with receiving the approval of outsiders. It was enough for them to enjoy the friendship that characterized the sect and provided the basis for the community's means of support.[59] Friends would naturally share what they possessed. Epicureans were severely criticized in antiquity, partly for their withdrawal from and disregard for society. They were accused of being haters of mankind and not the philanthropists they claimed to be.[60]

In the context of the social quietism and friendship of the Epicurean sect, and society's criticism of it, Paul's advice in

57. Philodemus *Peri Oikodomias* 23 (p. 64, ll. 7–18) in the Jensen edition. The translation quoted is that of A. J. Festugiere, *Personal Religion among the Greeks* (Los Angeles, 1954), 56.
58. See A. J. Festugiere, *Epicurus and His Gods*, trans. C. W. Chilton (Cambridge, Mass., 1956), Chap. 3. Quietism was not confined to the Epicureans. The temptation to retire from public life was particularly great in the first century. *Cf.*, MacMullen, *Enemies of the Roman Order*, Chap. 2. Discussion of *hesychia* was a commonplace; see Friedrick Wilhelm, "Plutarchos *Peri Hesychias*," *Rheinisches Museum*, LXXIII (1924), 466–82, for a collection of the evidence. However, the combination of friendship and retirement was associated in a special way with the Epicureans and was one of the attractions the sect may have had; *cf.*, Festugiere, *Personal Religion among the Greeks*, 50.
59. See Rolf Westman, *Plutarch gegen Kolotes* (Helsingfors, Finland, 1955), 226, and especially Norman W. de Witt, "The Epicurean Doctrine of Gratitude," *American Journal of Philology*, LVII (1937), 320–28.
60. For example, Plutarch's anti-Epicurean tracts, *That Epicurus Actually Makes a Pleasant Life Impossible, Reply to Colotes* and *Is "Live Unknown" a Wise Precept?*

I Thessalonians 4:9–12 takes on added significance. Having earlier presented himself to his converts as their model, working while he fulfilled his religious task, he now urges them to do the same: "Concerning love of the brethren you have no need to have any one write to you, for you yourselves have been taught by God to love one another; and indeed you do love all the brethren throughout Macedonia. But we exhort you to do so more and more, to aspire to live quietly (*hesychazein*), to mind your own affairs, and to work with your hands as we charged you; so that you may command the respect of outsiders, and be dependent on nobody." Like the Epicureans, the Christians in Thessalonica constituted a minority group, and they must have been tempted to assume a similar posture toward society. Significantly, Christianity was associated with Epicureanism by pagan critics later in the church's history. From the standpoint of an outsider Christianity and Epicureanism appeared similar in may respects: They were considered to be atheistic, misanthropic, socially irresponsible, and immoral.[61]

The Thessalonians may not have organized themselves along the lines of an Epicurean community or consciously adopted the Epicureans' view of their relationship to society, although that may indeed have been the case. Whether Paul's advice does reflect the actual situation in Thessalonica depends on two considerations: whether paraenesis can be taken to say something about the actual circumstances of the persons to whom it is addressed, or whether its tendency to be advice of

61. See Richard Jungkuntz, "Fathers, Heretics and Epicureans," *Journal of Ecclesiastical History*, XVII (1966), 3–10; A. D. Simpson, "Epicureans, Christians, Atheists in the Second Century," *Transactions of the American Philological Association*, LXXII (1941), 372–81. N..W. de Witt, *Epicurus and His Philosophy* (Minneapolis, 1954), 336ff., and especially *St. Paul and Epicurus* (Minneapolis, 1954); de Witt's exaggeration of the similarities should not obscure the fact that they did exist. See also A. R. Neumann, "Epikuros," Pauly-Wissowa, *Realenzyklopädie*, Supplementary Vol. XI (1968), 648.

universal applicability rules out such an assumption. [62] Should Paul have in mind specific problems in Thessalonica, questions remain whether the Thessalonians viewed themselves as analogous to the Epicurean communities, or whether Paul, by using the language he does, wishes to preclude that option to them. He may have detected tendencies in them that he felt were incongruent with the gospel and would lead to such criticism of the church as was leveled at the Epicureans. But Paul has a more positive view of society. He respects its opinion and wants that opinion to be formed in response to the church's conduct, which is governed by God's teaching. Paul must here refer to his own ministry, which he had fulfilled in word and deed (I Thess. 2:13f.; cf., 1:4ff.). How compelling his appeal was to the Thessalonians is not clear. We must be content only with Paul's view of the matter. If one accepts II Thessalonians as genuine, Paul would appear to have failed in his effort to convince all the members of that church (cf., II Thess. 3:6–15).

Paul's references to his manual labor in his Corinthian correspondence occur in apologetic contexts, which further suggests that his view of the matter was not the prevailing one in his churches (I Cor. 4:12; 9; II Cor. 11:7–11). These passages have in recent years been examined especially for information about the self-understanding of Paul and his opponents. Since we have more data on the interchange of ideas between Paul and the Corinthians than between him and the Thessalonians, further investigation of that church in light of other contemporary conventicles such as the Epicureans may help us to better understand his letters.

---

62. For example, David G. Bradley, "The *Topos* as a Form in the Pauline Paraenesis," *Journal of Biblical Literature*, LXXII (1953), 238–46. For a contrasting viewpoint, see Karl P. Donfried, "False Presuppositions in the Study of Romans," *Catholic Biblical Quarterly*, XXXVI (1974), esp. 341.

The approach I have here advocated began by identifying the type of literature represented by I Thessalonians as paraenetic. Examination of popular philosophical paraenesis revealed self-descriptions of the adviser and a concern for his relationship to his advisees similar to those found in I Thessalonians. I further inquired about the internal relationships of philosophical communities and about their attitude toward society, matters with which I Thessalonians is concerned. The issues were treated at great length in connection with the Epicureans, a philosophical school at times associated with early Christians in antiquity. The approach has its limitations in enabling us to determine the historical situation of the Thessalonian church, but it does appear successful in bringing to light social attitudes and issues that may have been important to the Thessalonians and that certainly were to Paul.

Paul *Papyrus*
letters
Judge + Deissman
2nd *1st*
in chapter.

2
Social Level and
Literary Culture

Ancient letters

ATTEMPTS to establish the social level of early Christians
invariably rest to a considerable degree on Paul's description of
his converts in Corinth (I Cor. 1:26): "For consider your call,
brethren; not many of you were wise according to worldly
standards, not many were powerful, not many were of noble
birth." Recent studies have stressed that this passage reveals
that the Corinthian church counted among its members at
least an influential minority of well-to-do persons, as well as a
large number of people from the lower classes.

Regarding the passage, E. A. Judge argues that these words
at face value "merely imply that the group did not contain
many intellectuals, politicians, or persons of gentle birth. But
this would suggest that the group did at least draw upon this
minority to some extent." [1] They represented the owner and
patron class that sponsored Christianity and had dependents
who were also converts. "But the dependent members of the
city households were by no means the most debased section of

1. E. A. Judge, *The Social Pattern of Christian Groups in the First Century* (London, 1960), 59. Gerd Theissen, whose views will be examined in Chap. 3, follows
up Judge's assessment, with some modifications.

29

society. If lacking freedom, they still enjoyed security, and a moderate prosperity. The peasantry and persons in slavery on the land were the most underprivileged classes. Christianity left them largely untouched."[2] It was the domination of a socially pretentious section of the population that was responsible for many of the church's problems.

Wilhelm Wuellner has recently come to similar conclusions through a different approach. After subjecting I Corinthians 1:26–28 to critical analysis of grammar and form, he suspects that "inferences drawn from archaeological sources notwithstanding, the Corinthian Christians came by and large from fairly well-to-do bourgeois circles with a fair percentage also from upper class people as well as the very poor. But to use I Corinthians 1:26–28 as the most important text in the whole New Testament for allegations of Christianity's proletarian origins is indefensible and no longer tenable simply and chiefly on grammatical grounds."[3]

Somewhat less significant are those attempts to describe the social constitution of early Christianity on the basis of the Acts of the Apostles and other late writings of the New Testament, which have a recognized tendency to describe Christianity as "middle class."[4] Heinz Kreissig seeks to correct what he considers to be an erroneous view of the social status of Christians

2. *Ibid.*, 60.

3. Wilhelm Wuellner, "The Sociological Implications of I Corinthians 1:26–28 Reconsidered," *Studia Evangelica*, IV, Vol. CXII of *Texte und Untersuchungen* (Berlin, 1973), 666–72.

4. For Luke's pride in the high social standing of Paul's converts, see Henry J. Cadbury, *The Book of Acts in History* (New York, 1955), 43; Eckhard Plümacher, *Lukas als hellenistischer Schriftsteller* (Göttingen, Germany, 1972), 22ff., 26, 30. On Luke's interest in women from the upper classes, see Martin Hengel, "Maria Magdalena und die Frauen als Zeugen," in Otto Betz, Martin Hengel, and Peter Schmidt (eds.), *Abraham unser Vater: Festschrift für Otto Michel* (Leiden, Holland, 1963), 243–56. Note also his interest in the "God-fearers" or "worshipers of God," who were generally of higher social status than proselytes. *Cf.*, Peter Stuhlmacher, *Das paulinische Evangelium* (Göttingen, Germany, 1968), I, 99 *n.* 5, 261; Henneke Gülzow, *Christentum und Sklaverei in den ersten drei Jahrhunderten* (Bonn, 1969), 13f.

in the first century. [5] Basing his study largely on Acts, the Pastoral Epistles, and the Shepherd of Hermas (!), he finds that Christianity did not grow so much among the proletariat or manual workers or small farmers as it did in urban circles of well-situated artisans and tradespeople. He admits that some Christians were poor or were slaves but cautions us that conversions of people from the upper ranks were not the exception. Kreissig does not mean that there were no revolutionary elements in early Christianity—it would still have to be determined to what social strata such "progressives" belonged.

I

It appears from the recent concern of scholars with the social level of early Christians, that a new consensus may be emerging. This consensus, if it is not premature to speak of one, is quite different from the one represented by Adolf Deissmann, which has held sway since the beginning of the century. [6] The more recent scholarship has shown that the social status of early Christians may be higher than Deissmann had supposed.

We have noted Karl Kautsky's opinion that in its beginnings Christianity was a movement among various unpropertied classes. Even those who opposed his Marxist interpretation agreed with his reading of the evidence. [7] In a review of Kautsky's book on the origins of Christianity, Deissmann did not

5. Heinz Kreissig, "Zur sozialen Zusammensetzung der frühchristlichen Gemeinden im ersten Jahrhundert u. Z.," *Eirene*, VI (1967), 91–100.
6. For the old view, see the survey of opinions, *ibid.*, 91–96. This view is still held by John C. Gager, *Kingdom and Community: The Social World of Early Christianity* (Englewood Cliffs, N.J., 1975), 96ff., 106ff. A major exception was Rudolf Schumacher, *Die soziale Lage der Christen im apostolischen Zeitalter* (Paderborn, Germany, 1924). See also K. Schreiner, "Zur biblischen Legitimation des Adels: Auslegungsgeschichte zu 1. Kor. 1, 26–29," *Zeitschrift für Kirchengeschichte*, LXXXV (1975), 317–57.
7. Other scholars also agreed about the social level of the earliest Christians but denied that they had any proletarian consciousness. *Cf.*, Martin Dibelius, *Urchristentum und Kultur* (Heidelberg, Germany, 1928), 20f., and the earlier literature cited by Schumacher, *Die soziale Lage der Christen.*

criticize him for his evaluation of the evidence but for his failure to appreciate the movement and the literature from below. Kautsky is accused of judging the Christian sources "not from the level of his own fundamental conception, but from that of a sated Berlin rationalism which looks down genteelly and unhistorically" upon the gospels and misses the character of Paul's letters. Kautsky had argued against the conception of Christianity as the creation of Jesus on the basis of the fact that Roman historians of the early Empire scarcely mention Jesus. In a statement that reflects his own romantic view of things, Deissmann answers: "This non-mention is the direct result of the specifically non-literary nature of Primitive Christianity—a movement among the weary and heavy-laden, men without power and position, 'babes' as Jesus himself calls them, the poor, the base, the foolish, as St. Paul with a prophet's sympathy decribes them. Kautsky himself knows the passage."[8]

Deissmann clearly believes in a correlation between social class and literary culture. His great work, *Light from the Ancient East*, which has influenced New Testament scholarship's understanding of the character of New Testament language and literature, is based on that presupposition. Deissmann was one of the most successful in convincing the scholarly community that the newly found papyri were important for understanding the New Testament. Complaining that most of the extant literature of antiquity represents the cultivated upper class, which almost always had been identified with the whole ancient world of the Imperial age, he welcomed the discovery of the papyri. These scraps from the rubbish heaps of antiquity opened our eyes to the common people, those classes from which "we have to think of the apostle Paul and the early

8. Adolf Deissmann, *Light from the Ancient East*, trans. Lionel R. M. Strachan (4th ed.; Grand Rapids, Mich., 1965), 466.

Christians gathering recruits."[9] Deissmann believes that these nonliterary documents are valuable for three reasons: 1) They guide us toward an accurate philological estimate of the New Testament and primitive Christianity; 2) they direct us to a correct literary appreciation of the New Testament; and 3) they provide us with information on social and religious history, "helping us to understand both the contact and the contrast between Primitive Christianity and the ancient world."[10]

New Testament language and literature formed part of Deissmann's understanding of the social character of early Christianity. Modifications have been made to Deissmann's assessment of the language and literature of the New Testament; but their implications for the social status of early Christianity have not been recognized. The purpose of this chapter, then, is to observe what research since Deissmann has taught us about the linguistic and literary character of the New Testament. In examining the level of literary culture of the New Testament, I do not wish to imply that the social level of early Christianity can be established solely on the basis of linguistic or literary data, which only complement other kinds of evidence at our disposal. Nor do I wish to suggest that all New Testament writers represent the same literary finesse. Deissmann, in basing his case primarily on the Gospels and Paul, utilized only those authors and those features in their works that generally represent most of the New Testament. He was fully aware that Luke and the author of Hebrews were purposely edging toward producing literary works for higher circles.

Paul is of special interest and warrants a brief digression before we turn to linguistic and literary considerations. His letters are the earliest New Testament writings and were ad-

9. Ibid., 9.
10. Ibid., 10.

dressed to actual situations in his mission churches. They are, therefore, valuable sources for learning about the churches. They also provide evidence about the man who wrote them, raising the issue of Paul's education.

The Church Fathers, measuring Paul by the criteria of classicism, were embarrassed by his rudeness of style. That, however, has not deterred his admirers in every generation from producing volumes on his erudition. [11] In justifying their attempts to portray his familiarity with Greek philosophy, these admirers frequently had recourse to the fact that he was born in Tarsus, one of the three major university cities of antiquity. Tarsus was known for the unusual involvement of its local populace in the academic enterprise. As a youth, they argued, Paul received a good Greek education that enabled him in later years to communicate with the philosophers in Athens. However, a detailed study of Acts 22:3 in light of similar contemporary descriptions of individuals' educational careers, has convinced W. C. van Unnik[12] that this passage should be punctuated as follows: "I am a Jew, born at Tarsus in Cilicia, but brought up in this city, educated at the feet of Gamaliel according to the strict manner of the law of our fathers, being zealous for God as you all are this day." According to this reading, Paul would already have spent his early youth in Jerusalem before he entered Gamaliel's school around the age of fifteen. His earliest formation could then be regarded as Jewish, taking place in an Aramaic-speaking community and determining his thought throughout his life. But to base either conclusion on the statement in Acts 22:3 is precarious. An earlier youth in Tarsus would not have guaranteed a thorough Greek education, nor would an early youth in Jerusalem have pre-

11. See Eduard Norden, *Die Antike Kunstprosa* (2 vols.; 2nd ed.; Leipzig, Germany, 1909; repr. Darmstadt, 1958), II, 491ff.; E. A. Judge, "St. Paul and Classical Society," *Jahrbuch für Antike und Christentum*, XV (1972), 29ff.

12. W. C. van Unnik, *Tarsus or Jerusalem? The City of Paul's Youth*, trans. G. Ogg (London, 1962).

cluded one. The Hellenization of Palestine was more thorough than has been thought, even to the extent that disciples of the rabbis were educated in Greek philosophy and rhetoric. It is of biographical interest to know where Paul received his education, but it is not of decisive importance in order to determine what his educational level was in the period of his greatest missionary activity, some twenty years after his conversion. By then he had spent two decades in a Greek environment—ample time for him to have assimilated the Greek culture that is reflected in his letters. His letters provide that primary information about the questions with which we are concerned, and it is to them and the other documents in the New Testament that we must turn.

II

Deissmann's major contribution was in the field of lexicography. [13] Reacting against the view that the New Testament was written in a language of its own, a "Holy Spirit Greek," he compared New Testament vocabulary with the newly discovered papyri and concluded that "for the most part, the pages of our sacred Book are so many records of popular Greek, in its various grades; taken as a whole the New Testament is a Book of the people." [14] Deissmann's immediate followers carried his work into the field of grammar, with the assurance "that the papyri have finally destroyed the figment of a New Testament Greek which is in any material respect different from that spoken by ordinary people in daily life throughout the Roman world." [15] The presence of Semitic elements in the New Testament writings posed problems for this theory, but these ele-

13. For a history of New Testament lexicography, see Gerhard Friedrich, "Zur Vorgeschichte des Theologischen Wörterbuchs zum Neuen Testament," in *Theologisches Wörterbuch zum Neuen Testament*, X (1974), 1–52.
14. Deissmann, *Light from the Ancient East*, 143.
15. James Hope Moulton, *A Grammar of New Testament Greek, I: Prolegomena* (3 vols.; Edinburgh, 1906), 18f.

ments were explained as literal translations of the Old Testament and Aramaic sources that did not constitute sufficient reason for isolating the language of the New Testament.

Recent writers have not been satisfied with that explanation, for the features under discussion occur "in parts of the New Testament where the possibility of Semitic sources is more than remote." Instead, the distinctive features have been attributed to the familiarity of Christian writers with the Septuagint. It is further held by Nigel Turner, who has produced the most extensive recent work on the syntax of New Testament Greek, "that the language of the Old Testament translators and the New Testament writers was the same: a living dialect of Jewish Greek," a unique language with a character and unity of its own.[16] As such it should be classified as a distinct type of the common Greek. "It belongs neither to the popular papyrus texts nor to the cultured exponents of what is called the literary *Koine*. Biblical Greek is far removed from the uncultured dialect of the marketplace. Greek-speaking Jews had imbibed their linguistic tradition from religious experience, from the bilingual necessity which was forced upon them, and most of all from the study of the Greek Old Testament and from synagogue worship."[17] By no means do all linguists accept Turner's view that New Testament Greek is a special dialect,[18] but the Semitic element is generally admitted to be more significant than Deissmann and his immediate successors had thought.

The sociological implications of this shift in opinion must

16. Nigel Turner, "Second Thoughts: Papyrus Finds," *Expository Times*, LXXVI (1964), 45. See also his *A Grammar of New Testament Greek, III: Syntax* (3 vols.; Edinburgh, 1963), and *cf.*, Klaus Beyer, *Semitische Syntax im Neuen Testament* (Göttingen, Germany, 1962).

17. Turner, "Second Thoughts," 46.

18. *Cf.*, Edgar V. McKnight, "The New Testament and 'Biblical' Greek," *Journal of Bible and Religion*, XXXIV (1966), 36–42.

still be determined. Three decades before the publication of Turner's book, A. D. Nock was also impressed by the differences between the language, especially the vocabulary, of the papyri and of Paul:

> Any man who knows his classical Greek authors and reads the New Testament and then looks into the papyri is astonished at the similarities which he finds. Any man who knows the papyri first and then turns to Paul is astonished at the differences. There has been much exaggeration of the Koine element in the New Testament. . . . Nothing could be less like the Pauline letters than the majority of the documents in Deissmann's *Light from the Ancient East*. Paul is not writing peasant Greek or soldier Greek; he is writing the Greek of a man who has the Septuagint in his blood.[19]

The Septuagint and the New Testament have vocabulary and usages that would have been strange to a Greek. Such usages, Nock points out, "are the product of an enclosed world living its own life, a ghetto culturally and linguistically if not geographically; they belong to a literature written entirely for the initiated, like the magic papyri with their technical use of such words as *ousia, sustasis, agoge*. Philosophical works intended for wider circles had some peculiar turns of speech and words, *proegmena*, for instance, but they bore a meaning on the surface. Writings which did not satisfy this requirement could not and did not court publicity outside the movement."[20] Thus, whereas Deissmann had seen the sociological value of New Testament Greek as placing Christianity on the social scale, Nock suggests that the value of the language lies in its reflection of the in-group mentality of the early Christians. It appears that the more New Testament Greek emerges as a dis-

---

19. A. D. Nock, "The Vocabulary of the New Testament," *Journal of Biblical Literature*, LII (1933), 138f., most readily accessible in Zeph Stewart (ed.), *Essays on Religion and the Ancient World* (2 vols.; Cambridge, Mass., 1972), I, 346f.

20. Nock, "The Vocabulary of the New Testament," 135, or Stewart, *Essays on Religion and the Ancient World*, 344.

-tinct type by virtue of its Semitic character, the more it reveals the mind-set of a minority group; and this perception is relevant to the current interest in early Christian communities. Investigation of the sociological significance of this in-group Greek will have to deal with the fact that, although we cannot absolutely deny the possibility of pagan analogies, "apart from the magic papyri, which are working copies for use, we have no writings of men of esoteric piety addressed only to their spiritual brethren. It may be questioned whether many such existed."[21] This is, therefore, an instance in which the riches of our Christian sources may enable us to cast light on other ancient cults. Nevertheless, examination of the phenomenon should take into consideration ancient[22] and modern[23] occurrences that may appear in some way analogous, as well as the insight offered by the social sciences.[24]

The style of New Testament Greek has also been perceived

21. *Ibid.*
22. The Hellenistic Pythagoreans' adoption of the Doric dialect, in addition to the linguistic phenomena mentioned by Nock, remains a tantalizing enigma that may deserve further attention. Holger Thesleff thinks that these "somewhat reactionary Academic and Peripatetic propaganda" pieces were aimed at a select public, which was expected to listen, and that they are clearly not esoteric, but "semi-exoteric." *Cf.*, Thesleff's "On the Problem of the Doric Pseudo-Pythagorica: An Alternative Theory of Date and Purpose," in *Pseudepigrapha*, I, 85f., in *Entretiens sur l'antiquité classique* (Vandoeuvres-Geneva, 1971), Vol. XVIII of the Fondation Hardt Series, and his earlier work, *An Introduction to the Pythagorean Writings of the Hellenistic Period* (Abo, Finland, 1961), 77ff. If they were "semi-exoteric," their archaistic Doric garb might be explained partially by their intention to show the debt of Plato and Aristotle to Pythagoras. But the Pythagoreans were not merely scoring a polemical point, for they sincerely believed that the debt was real. Therefore the adoption of Doric in these tractates also reflects on the Pythagoreans themselves.
23. The Quaker plain speech may be a case in point. The use of *thee* and *thou*, "though it originated in the intention to treat all men as equals, has turned out in practice to establish a new distinction," Henry J. Cadbury, *Friendly Heritage* (Norwalk, Conn., 1972), 241. It is one of their customs that has become "a badge of peculiarity for a sect," Hugh Barbour, *The Quakers in Puritan England* (New Haven, Conn., 1964), 241.
24. Suggestive is Wayne A. Meeks, "The Man from Heaven in Johannine Sectarianism," *Journal of Biblical Literature*, XCII (1972), 46–72.

by other scholars to be different from that of the man in the street. Albert Wifstrand argues that Hebrews, James, and I Peter have characteristics quite different from the vernacular.[25] Deissmann had recognized that these letters were more literary than those of Paul, but Wifstrand tries to evaluate their style more precisely. He states that the obvious differences between their style and the vernacular are the special words and religious terms in the New Testament. But he notes that even in comparison with the Hellenistic diatribe, with which many points of contact have been seen, the New Testament makes much greater use of metaphor and abstract nouns and is far more intimate. The language of these letters is not vulgar, but is the ordinary *Koine* written by people of some education. It shows the predilections of Hellenistic secretarial and scientific prose and also the use of the Semitic by the authors when they wished to write in a higher style. It therefore appears to be a language of the Hellenized synagogue, which is not, however, a special dialect. Its phonology, syntax, and accidence and formation of sentences show a preference for Semitic modes of expression.

Wifstrand does not claim this preference for all the writings of the New Testament, but it is important that he perceives a combination of professional prose and the Semitized language of the synagogue. Also significant is his relation of the character of New Testament Greek to the Christian community:

What is peculiar to the New Testament is that God is nearer and one's fellowmen are nearer than they are to the Jews and Greeks, the conception of community has quite another importance, the valuations are more intense, and for that reason the emotionally tinged adjectives too are more frequent (dear, precious, glorious, living, everlasting, imperishable, and so on) together with other stylistic fea-

25. Albert Wifstrand, "Stylistic Problems in the Epistles of James and Peter," *Studia Theologica*, I (1948), 170–82.

tures which appear in almost all late Christian preaching, but often in so empty and humdrum a manner that there is reason to wish for a little less of New Testament expression and a little more of New Testament spirit.[26]

Wifstrand's notion of professional prose was taken up by his student Lars Rydbeck.[27] Rydbeck does not deny the Semitic coloring in New Testament Greek, but he insists that one should always try to determine whether those elements also appear in professional prose of the period. He bases his understanding of that style on technical writings on philology (Didymus), pharmacology (Dioscurides), technology (Heron), mathematics (Nichomachus), and astronomy (Ptolemaeus). These writers, who were interested in communicating facts and had no belletristic aims, wrote a nonliterary, nonclassical prose. This was the standard language used by people when they wished to express themselves without any literary pretension. It was also the style taught in schools and learned by people whose home language was not Greek. But we cannot assume that it was the common *spoken* language. The vernacular that

26. *Ibid.*, 182. Pagans took offense at the intimacy Christians felt among themselves and expressed in their language, for example, their description of themselves as brothers. See the reflection of pagan views in Tertullian *Apology* 39, and Minucius Felix *Octavius* 9:2; 31:8, and on the latter *cf.*, *The Octavius of Marcus Minucius Felix*, trans. and annotated by Graeme W. Clarke (New York, 1974), notes 116 and 528. See also Lucian *Peregrinus* 13 and Hans Dieter Betz, "Lukian von Samosata und das Christentum," *Novum Testamentum*, III (1959), 233f. Betz's suggestion that Lucian is simply describing early Christians in terms of a common Hellenistic ideal does not sufficiently consider the polemical nature of the pagan concern with the description of Christians as brothers, or the special connotations of the term. The significant work of Christine Mohrmann and her students has demonstrated how Christian Greek and Latin, especially of the later period, transformed the meaning words originally had in pagan usage. See. G. J. M. Bartelink, "Umdeutung heidnischer Termini im christlichen Sprachgebrauch," in *Die Alte Kirche* (Munich, 1974), 397–418, and the literature cited there, Vol. I of Heinzgünter Frohnes and Uwe V. Knorr (eds.), *Kirchengeschichte als Missionsgeschichte* (Munich, 1974), 397–418.
27. Lars Rydbeck, *Fachprosa, vermeintliche Volkssprache und Neues Testament* (Uppsala, Sweden, 1967).

Deissmann found in most of the papyri is actually found in only a small percentage of the total papyrus documents, and our knowledge of it is still very limited. The language of the New Testament, according to Rydbeck, is the written language of educated people, not that of the vulgar papyri. Although he does not draw any sociological conclusions, his findings agree with the presently emerging view of the higher social status of early Christians.[28]

III

Some scholars have thought that the quotations of and the allusions to classical Greek authors in the New Testament may be an indication of the literary culture of the writers who used them.[29] Several allusions of a proverbial nature do occur, which, on the surface, have parallels in classical literature:[30] "The love of money is the root of all evils" (I Tim. 6:10); "Why do you seek the speck that is in your brother's eye but do not notice the log that is in your own eye?" (Matt. 7:3); "Physician, heal yourself" (Luke 4:23); "Having eyes do you not see, and having ears do you not hear?" (Mark 8:18); and "The dog turns back to his own vomit, and the sow is washed in the mire" (II

28. Almost half of Rydbeck's references are to Luke and Acts of the Apostles, which are hardly representative of New Testament Greek.

29. Deissmann does not deal with them because of his conviction that the New Testament is nonliterary. Cf., Norden, *Die antike Kunstprosa*, II, 498, on Paul. E. B. Howell, "St. Paul and the Greek World," *Greece and Rome*, 2nd ser., XI (1964), 7–29. (A shorter version appears in *Expository Times*, LXXI [1960], 328–32.) Howell argues that Paul was indebted to Plato; that he "quoted or echoed classical authors more freely than is usually allowed"; and that, in short, "he was a complete member of the Greek world, or rather that he could and did assume that character when it suited his purpose to do so" (p. 8). Howell is corrected by H. R. Minn, "Classical Reminiscence in St. Paul," *Prudentia*, VI (1974), 93–98.

30. See the excellent treatment of the subject by Robert Renehan, "Classical Greek Quotations in the New Testament," in David Neiman and Margaret Schatkin (eds.), *The Heritage of the Early Church: Essays in Honor of the Very Reverend Georges Vasilievich Florovsky* (Rome, 1973), 17–45, to which I am indebted for much of what follows.

Pet. 2:22). Closer scrutiny reveals that, rather than being derived from Greek literature, these allusions come from widespread sapiential traditions. Furthermore, the background of some of them is the Old Testament and Jewish writings. Since morals are expressed in terms of popular wisdom that knows few cultural boundaries, it is not surprising that the Greeks also expressed the same thoughts.[31]

There is another group of statements that may indeed go back to classical authors, especially to the tragedian Euripides. "You might find yourself fighting against God" (Acts 5:39) and "It hurts to kick against the goads" (Acts 26:14) may have had their ultimate origin in the *Bacchae*. Other echoes from Euripides have also been advanced as evidence that Luke was familiar with that author.[32] But that is not a necessary conclusion. Long before the first century, verses from Euripides were systematically collected and later found in anthologies designed for use in schools.[33] Quotations of such verses without any attribution of authorship does not, therefore, verify a personal reading of the original author.

A few exact quotations from Greek authors, however, do appear in Paul or are attributed to him. Paul's caution that "bad company ruins good morals" (I Cor. 15:33) may have come from one of Menander's plays, as critical editions of the New Testament indicate; but it is likely that Menander himself had borrowed it from Euripides.[34] In any case, the quotation has a proverbial character that was a feature of many quotations appearing in the Hellenistic diatribe, the style here adopted by

31. The Golden Rule is a good example. See A. Dihle, *Die goldene Regel: Eine Einführung in die Geschichte der antiken und frühchristlichen Vulgärethik* (Göttingen, Germany, 1962).

32. For the most important bibliography, see P. W. van der Horst, "Drohund und Mord schnaubend (Acta ix.1)," *Novum Testamentum*, XII (1970), 265 n. 2.

33. *Cf.* Bruno Snell, *Scenes from Greek Drama* (Los Angeles, 1964), 51 n. 4.

34. See Frederick W. Danker, "Menander and the New Testament," *New Testament Studies*, X (1964), 365–68; H. B. Rosén, "Motifs and *Topoi* from the New Comedy in the New Testament?" *Ancient Society*, III (1972), 245–57.

Paul.[35] He shows no awareness of the author from whom it originally came. In Titus 1:12 the statement, "Cretans are always liars, evil beasts, lazy gluttons," is attributed by the author to "a prophet of their own." He may have had Epimenides, who was a Cretan, in mind. But this statement, too, had become proverbial by the first century A.D. and is insufficient evidence of a firsthand knowledge of the works of Epimenides (sixth century B.C.). Epimenides has also been suggested as the author of the first quotation attributed to Paul in Acts 17:28, "In him we live and move and have our being," to which a quotation from Aratus, "For we are indeed his offspring," is added. Whether these two quotations have been accurately ascribed has been discussed at great length. It is sufficient for our purposes to note that the thought expressed by the two quotations is that of a widely diffused Stoicism, and that the latter quotation from Aratus (fourth–third century B.C.) appears in a poem on astronomy that enjoyed great popularity in antiquity. Thus we are once more brought to a level on which handbooks, anthologies, and summaries were used.

These classical allusions and quotations do, however, reflect a certain level of literary culture. The writings of Hellenistic authors, especially those of the moral philosophers, teem with quotations of this type. What the Hellenistic age lacked in originality it sought to make up by repeating and applying the wisdom of classical writers.[36] But those writers were not always read in their entirety. The schools had recourse to selections from classical works, which were frequently arranged according to moral topics.[37] The massive work of Stobaeus provides an excellent example of such collections. Rather than

35. See Abraham J. Malherbe, "The Beasts at Ephesus," *Journal of Biblical Literature*, LXXXVII (1968), 71–80.
36. On the moral aspect of the study of the poets, see H. I. Marrou, *A History of Education in Antiquity*, trans. George Lamb (New York, 1956), 234f.
37. See Henry Chadwick, "Florilegium," *Reallexikon für Antike und Christentum*, VII (1969), 1131–60.

read the works of classical philosophers firsthand, students generally learned their philosophy from handbooks that summarized or compared the doctrines of the different schools. Handbooks provided an introduction for most secondary-school students to subjects ranging from rhetoric to land surveying.[38]

Rhetoricians nevertheless supplied reading lists for their students in which the works of Euripides and Menander are frequently recommended.[39] Quintilian provided lists for young students who were preparing for the bar (*Institutio Oratoria* X, 1, 67f.), and Dio Chrysostom did the same for a mature individual who wished to take part in public life but had no time or inclination to subject himself to a more formal education (*Oration* 18:6f.). Recommending these authors proved useful for the man in public life rather than for developing literary appreciation. Of Euripides, Dio says, "He cleverly fills his plays with an abundance of characters and moving incidents, and strews them with maxims useful on all occasions, since he was not without acquaintance with philosophy." This practical interest was responsible for the collections of statements from the poets, which were used by most students. What was important was the wisdom contained in the poems, not their authorship, and they could be quoted without any attribution of authorship. Moral philosophers, who attempted to reform the masses, used these sayings because they believed the poets were the authorities of the masses and representatives of the common wisdom. By quoting proverbial statements from poets, a teacher could assume that they expressed "the thought and feeling of men generally, just what the many think about wealth and the other objects of their admiration, and what

---

38. See Ilona Opelt, "Epitome," *Reallexikon für Antike und Christentum*, V (1962), 944–73.

39. Papyrus finds also testify to the relative popularity of the two authors. See Plümacher, *Lukas als hellenistischer Schriftsteller*, 28f.

they consider would be the greatest good derived from each of them" (Dio, *Oration* 7:98).[40]

The quotations and allusions in the New Testament all demonstrate this level of literary culture in which the practical rather than aesthetic interests dominated. In addition, they help us to establish the lowest educational level that can reasonably be assumed for the New Testament writers who use them, *i.e.*, the upper levels of secondary-school instruction.[41]

IV

Allusions to the classics do more than point to the educational level of the New Testament writers; they may have implications for the scholastic aspect of early Christian communities. I here distinguish scholastic activity from the educational system I have described. The scholastic activity of which I speak presupposes an educational level that would have made "academic" activity possible. According to E. A. Judge we need not know only what relation Christians as a group had to the social structure of their own communities, "but what they existed for as a group, what activities they engaged in, and what their contemporaries would have made of them."[42] Although the churches could be classified in terms of their cultic or social welfare activities, Judge chooses to isolate them, especially the Pauline churches, as scholastic communities. He may be charged with overstating his case, but since he is one of the few professional social historians who has worked for decades in a field to which New Testament scholars have only recently returned, and since his views are not widely known in this

40. *Cf.*, Dio Chrysostom *Oration* 2:5.
41. *Cf.*, Marrou, *A History of Education in Antiquity*, 233–42.
42. E. A. Judge, "The Early Christians as a Scholastic Community," *Journal of Religious History*, 1 (1960–61), 8. See also Hans Conzelmann, "Paulus und die Weisheit," *New Testament Studies*, XII (1966), 231–44. Conzelmann hypothesized that Paul organized a school activity devoted to the study of "Wisdom."

country, it may be of value to introduce his thoughts in this context. His assessment of the social status of early Christians is markedly different from that of Deissmann.

Judge argues that the early churches "were founded and to some extent carried on under the auspices of professional preachers, which makes them parallel in some respects to the philosophical movements of the day."[43] Because of its academic character early Christianity is better known than are other religious movements. Indeed, he affirms, Christian literature is devoted almost entirely to this academic aspect of its affairs, so that we know far more about the churches' arguments over points of ethical and theological doctrine than we do about their religious practices. The missionary method of Paul serves to illustrate the phenomenon as Judge understands it.

He calls Paul a sophist, "without prejudice to the value or sincerity of his thought," in order to place him in his correct social class in terms of the impression his activities must have given to contemporary observers. The term *sophist*, for Judge's purposes, includes philosophers as well as the orators with whom the term is usually associated. All these men must have been more learned than their critics have shown. Judge surmises that Paul acquired the rhetorical art "by hard experience rather than by training. It was as his own profession, that of rabbi, failed him (when ejected from the synagogues), that he took up the new one."[44]

43. Judge, "The Early Christians as a Scholastic Community," 125. In his assessment Judge differs markedly from Gager, *Kingdom and Community*, 5, 106f., who regards the early Christians as nonintellectual in contrast to the later Gnostics. Judge, "St. Paul and Classical Society," 23, also registers his dissatisfaction with the History of Religions School for not appreciating Christianity's historical singularity.

44. Judge, "The Early Christians as a Scholastic Community," 127. Although Judge here considered it safe to "lump" Aelius Aristides and Dio Chrysostom with Epictetus, the Cynics, Apollonius of Tyana, and Peregrinus in the sophistic class to

Paul's Roman citizenship gave him status among the social elite of the Hellenistic states.[45] He moved in well-established circles where there was opportunity for vigorous discussion about behavior and ideas. This took place in privately organized meetings under the patronage of eminent persons, who also provided him with a retinue of assistants and an audience composed of their dependents. Judge identifies as many as forty persons who were supposed to have sponsored Paul's activities. They were all "persons of substance, members of a cultivated social elite."[46] Another class of approximately forty known persons constituted Paul's professional following. With Paul they traveled and did missionary work, remaining under his immediate control. These eighty people supplied the platform and retinue of Paul the sophist. "The importance of this for our picture of [the] social character of the Hellenistic churches is that it is only in this connection that we know of them, and that there is simply nobody else that we know of in any other connection of consequence in the churches."[47]

Judge's prosopography presents a stimulating case for regarding Paul in his social position as a sophist. He suggests some points that should receive further attention. Paul, unlike other touring preachers, "established a set of corporate societies independent of himself and yet linked to him by a constant traffic of delegations." Furthermore, Paul "is always anxious about the transmission of the *logos* and the acquisition

---

which Paul belonged (p. 126), he later excludes the Cynics on the grounds that they "were far too conspicuous and vulgar to do anything but repel people from the well-established circles in which Paul moved" (Judge, "St. Paul and Classical Society," 32.).

45. But note Judge's later comment that "Roman citizenship may not have been so decisive a status factor in the Greek cities of the first century as has been supposed" ("St. Paul and Classical Society," 25f.).

46. Judge, "The Early Christians as a Scholastic Community," 130.

47. *Ibid.*, 134f.

of *gnosis*. . . . The Christian faith, therefore, as Paul expands it, belongs with the doctrines of the philosophical schools rather than with the esoteric rituals of the mystery religions." This is shown especially by his concentration on ethics. The academic character of the Pauline communities emerged still more clearly when the interests of his rivals and peers were studied. Paul constantly attacks them on points of academic belief and moral practice, whereas "the religious activities of the Christian societies, the organization and the conduct of the cult are of only minor concern." Paul also denounces his opponents as sophists and dissociates himself from their method —actions that introduce the question of the exact function of rhetoric in Paul's ministry.[48]

This provocative outline shows that Paul's relationship with his churches seems to have no exact analogies elsewhere. But it is not clear that the churches were independent of him. If anything, Paul appears meddlesome, even if his churches do occasionally turn to him for advice. What is needed is a study of the role of the intermediaries between the two parties, as well as some inquiry into the sociological function of the letters, which are surrogates for Paul's presence.[49]

The contact between Paul and popular philosophy is most evident in the field of ethics.[50] For a proper perspective, however, we must have a more realistic understanding of both the unity and the diversity among philosophers of the day. We are accustomed to stressing the philosophical *Koine*, especially as

48. *Ibid.*, 135f.
49. See the discussion of I Thessalonians, pp. 22–27; *cf.* 15–16, 57–58 herein. A closer examination of epistolary paraenesis will aid in clarifying the relationship between the letter writers and their readers. On Seneca, see Hildegard Cancik, *Untersuchungen zu Senecas Epistulae Morales* (Hildesheim, Germany, 1967), Pt. 2, and Winfried Trillitzsch, *Senecas Beweisführung* (Berlin, 1962), 69f.
50. See Abraham J. Malherbe, "Hellenistic Moralists and the New Testament," in Hildegard Temporini (ed.), *Aufstieg und Niedergang der römischen Welt* (7 vols. to date; Berlin, 1976—). Vol. II, Pt. 3.

it touches on ethics, to the point that differences or contrary viewpoints blur, or disappear completely. This is regrettable, since it is precisely the differences that are significant for understanding some of the issues reflected in the New Testament. The discussion regarding Paul's custom of working to support himself is a case in point.[51] An appreciation of the diversity of practice and teaching among representatives of the same school should also guard us against rejecting philosophers whom we mistakenly identify with a type that cannot legitimately represent the whole school. For example, Judge's view of the Cynics as "far too conspicuous and vulgar to do anything but repel people from the well-established circles in which Paul moved"[52] reflects a view of the Cynics that is presented in many of Lucian's satires; but that view hardly comports with Lucian's view of Demonax, or with the writings of Dio Chrysostom, who, even during his Cynic period, could hardly have been accused of vulgarity.

Judge suggests that the concept of popular ethics may enable us to place Paul more securely in the society of his day. By popular ethics he does not mean "any systematic propagation of ideas to the public, such as the Cynics undertook, but the way in which a loose body of general principles for life develops amongst thoughtful people in a community."[53] Although the insights into popular ethics, gained especially by Albrecht Dihle,[54] are certainly valuable, we must have greater precision at this point if we are to move forward. If, by the Cynics' "systematic propagation of ideas," Judge refers to the types of paraenesis identified by form critics, and if he places a low value on them as important sources for our knowledge of the

51. See pp. 24–27 herein.
52. *Cf.*, p. 46 *n.* 44 herein.
53. Judge, "St. Paul and Classical Society," 32f.
54. For a summary and appreciation of Dihle's work by E. A. Judge, see "'Antike und Christentum': Some Recent Work from Cologne," *Prudentia*, V (1973), 1–7.

relationship between Christians and their society, I must disagree with his assessment.[55] The stock-in-trade of the Greek moralists, for example—the lists of vices and virtues, the moral commonplaces, the hortatory style—are all found in Paul and other New Testament writings and have been studied intensively.[56] But the stress has been on the origin and literary form of these devices rather than on their function. It is the function especially that should occupy us if we are to have a better understanding of Christian communities. An example of the type of approach that may produce rich dividends is provided by the *Haustafeln*, the lists of duties of members of a household.[57]

55. Judge's criticism of New Testament scholarship for reducing paraenesis to a formal type ("St. Paul and Classical Society," 33) suggests that this is the case, but his caution that New Testament scholars need to give more attention to the problems of definition and evidence of the diatribe has real merit. Criticisms by early reviewers of Rudolf Bultmann, *Der Stil der paulinischen Predigt und die kynisch-stoische Diatribe* (Göttingen, Germany, 1910), seem to have escaped most New Testament scholars. For a summary of these criticisms, see my comments in "Hellenistic Moralists and the New Testament." Judge believes that further work should map out the difference between the pagan and Christian diatribes: "The so-called diatribe, whether in its drastic Bionic form or in the more temperate work of Musonius and Epictetus, deals in commonplaces, delivered as a literary creation against stock targets. It lacks altogether the engagement with actual people, circumstances and disputed ideas that is characteristic of Paul." Further investigation will have to determine whether such a generalization holds for the pagan diatribes. Evidence suggests that there is a correlation between the style of the diatribes and the social setting in which they were delivered. The addresses of Maximus of Tyre to aristocratic circles in Rome are different from those of Epictetus to his students in a classroom, which again differ from those of Dio Chrysostom to the masses. We shall have to take more seriously the possibility that the discernible differences in form and style of what are known as diatribes are related to their sociological functions. On the diatribal factors in Paul's letter to Rome as reflecting a concrete situation, see Karl P. Donfried, "False Presuppositions in the Study of Romans," *Catholic Biblical Quarterly*, XXXVI (1974), 332–55.

56. See the bibliographies in Wolfgang Schrage, *Die konkrete Einzelgebote in der paulinischen Paränese* (Gütersloh, Germany, 1961); Ehrhard Kamlah, *Die Form der katalogischen Paränese im Neuen Testament* (Tübingen, Germany, 1964); James E. Crouch, *The Origin and Intention of the Colossian Haustafel* (Göttingen, Germany, 1972).

57. See Malherbe, "Hellenistic Moralists and the New Testament," and, for more detail, David L. Balch, "'Let Wives Be Submissive . . . ': The Origin, Form

Such lists were widely used in moral instruction in antiquity. Order in the household, which was viewed as a microcosm of society, was supposed to guarantee order in society as a whole. Instruction on how to behave toward the gods, the state, married partners, and to children assumed a recognizable form. Such lists appear in Hellenistic Jewish and Christian writings, and their implications regarding the inner life of the Christian communities have begun to receive scholarly attention.[58] But the lists have not been discussed in relation to the emerging picture of the house church. In addition to information that they may provide about the structure of such churches and the relationship between their various members, they should also be examined for evidence of the community's relationship with the larger society. Such possibilities demand that more attention be given to the function of the lists, particularly to their use by minority groups.

An immediate background to the New Testament use of the lists is provided by Hellenistic Judaism. Conversion to Judaism created tension between proselytes and their pagan associates and relatives. Philo, in encouraging Jews to give special consideration to proselytes, describes them as having turned their kinsfolk into mortal enemies by rejecting the myths so highly honored by their ancestors. The proselytes had left their country, their relatives, and their friends for the sake of virtue and religion. Recognizing the social disruption caused by their conversion, Philo urges that proselytes be made to feel at home in the divine society to which they had been called.[59] Their new allegiance and the sense of belonging provided by membership in an exclusive minority group did not go unnoticed by pagan observers who were scandalized by conversion to Juda-

---

and Apologetic Function of the Household Duty Code (*Haustafel*) in I Peter" (Ph.D. Dissertation, Yale University, 1974).

58. Crouch, *Origin and Intention*.

59. Philo *Special Laws* I, 52, and IV, 178.

ism. Of proselytes Tacitus the Roman historian says, "The earliest lesson they receive is to despise the gods, to disown their country, and to regard their parents, children, and brothers as of little account."[60] In other words, when describing what he believes to be the social irresponsibility of converts to Judaism, Tacitus uses the same categories that outline proper social behavior in the *Haustafeln*. One could expect that in response to such polemic an apology might be developed that would address itself to the charges or that might even use the *Haustafel* apologetically. The latter indeed appears to have been the case.

Both Philo and Josephus use expansions of the *Haustafel* form to counter the charges that Judaism was antisocial and to present it as the ideal society.[61] Such an apologetic use of the *Haustafel* can also be detected in I Peter. The community to which that letter was written was undergoing persecutions of an unofficial and social rather than legal character. The addressees are described as being spoken against (2:12), reviled (3:9), troubled (3:14), abused (4:4), and reproached (4:14). With full awareness of the tension between the Christians and their society, the author, using a *Haustafel*, exhorts them at length to continue in the Christian life. Actually, the *Haustafel* by this time had become a *Gemeindetafel*, a community list, in Christian use.

It has been argued that I Peter was written to Christians who had previously been God-fearers, and that Hellenistic Jewish writings dealing with proselytes contribute to the clarification of the letter.[62] The function of the *Haustafel* is illu-

---

60. Tacitus *Histories* V, 5.
61. Philo *Hypothetica*, preserved in Eusebius, *Preparation for the Gospel* VIII, 6 and 7, 355c–361b; Josephus *Against Apion* II, 190ff.
62. W. C. van Unnik, *De Verlossing I Petrus 1:18–19 en het Probleem van den eersten Petrusbrief, Mededeelingen der Nederlandsche Akademie van Wetenschappen, Afdeeling Letterkunde*, n.s., Pt. 5, No. 1 (Amsterdam, 1942).

minated by that insight. It is introduced with the command, "Maintain good conduct among the Gentiles, so that in case they speak against you as wrongdoers, they may see your good deeds and glorify God on the day of visitation" (2:12). The good conduct is then specified in a list of responsibilities toward governmental authorities (2:13ff.), of slaves to their masters (2:18ff.), of wives to their husbands (3:1ff.), of husbands to their wives (3:7), and of all Christians to each other (3:8f.). The apologetic and missionary functions, which were not separate from each other in Hellenistic Judaism, are combined in the introduction and in the detailed advice to slaves (2:15) and wives (3:1f.). While Christians are "aliens and exiles" in this world (2:11) and do form a brotherhood (2:17; 5:9), they are, nevertheless, a responsible part of society and represent a quality of life that is intelligible enough to outsiders to function as missionary witness and defense. When perceived in this manner, the _Haustafel_ is no longer simply a piece of standard Hellenistic moral exhortation that is Christianized here and there, as it is frequently thought to be; but it becomes an important piece of evidence for how the internal life of a Christian community, which had its own unique character, was seen as relating to a society that was suspicious of it.

To return to Judge's provocative outline, he suggests that the issues between Paul and his Christian rivals involved academic belief rather than religious practice. But it is not at all clear that the two were viewed as separate, either by Paul or his opponents, or that the debate was conducted as though they were separate.[63] However, Judge's bringing the philosophical movements of Paul's day into the discussion of how the early Christians' contemporaries perceived them has real merit, as my investigation of I Thessalonians has attempted to

63. _Cf._, p. 12 _n_. 28 herein.

53

show (Chap. 1). To Greeks, Judaism, with its emphasis on monotheism and morals, must have appeared to be a school of philosophy,[64] and Philo himself described the synagogue activity as a devotion to philosophy.[65] It is to be expected, therefore, that scholars would attempt to relate first-century Christianity to contemporary philosophical schools.[66] Such efforts would be worthwhile if care were exercised not to make generalizations on the basis of work done on the subject almost a century ago.

Judge is also correct in drawing attention to the importance of rhetorical practice. It was an issue between Paul and some of his churches, especially the one in Corinth, where his opponents laid hold of it to demonstrate the insufficiency of Paul's apostleship.[67] An awareness of the importance attached to it does tell us something of the educational, theological, and social values of at least some members of that church.

An awareness of ancient rhetorical theory and practice also brings important insights into Paul and his writings. There was a tendency among the Church Fathers and in German

64. George Foot Moore, *Judaism in the First Centuries of the Christian Era* (3 vols.; Cambridge, Mass., 1927), I, 284; A. D. Nock, *Conversion* (Oxford, 1933), 78; Werner Jaeger, *Early Christianity and Greek Paideia* (Cambridge, Mass., 1961), 29ff.

65. Philo *On Dreams* II, 127 and *On the Contemplative Life* 26. *Cf.*, also, Josephus' description of the Jewish sects in terms of philosophical schools, *War* II, 162–66; Josephus *Antiquities* XIII, 171–73, and XVIII, 11–17. One should beware of making a contrast between intellectual, *sc.*, philosophical discussion and religion as activities in which other organized communities would engage. For the cults and the schools, see Martin P. Nilsson, *Die hellenistische Schule* (Munich, 1955). For the spiritual exercises of the philosophical schools, see Paul Rabbow, *Seelenführung: Methodik der Exerzitien in der Antike* (Munich, 1954).

66. See Olof Linton, *Das Problem der Urkirche in den neueren Forschung* (Uppsala, Sweden, 1932), 31ff.

67. On the importance of rhetoric in I Corinthians, see Johannes Munck, *Paul and the Salvation of Mankind*, trans. Frank Clarke (London, 1959), esp. 148ff., and on Paul's opponents in II Corinthians, see the influential interpretation by Dieter Georgi, *Die Gegner des Paulus im 2. Korintherbrief* (Neukirchen-Vluyn, Germany, 1964).

classical scholarship around the turn of the century to take Paul's statement that he was "unskilled in speaking" (II Cor. 11:6) at face value and to compare him unfavorably with ancient rhetoricians.[68] To Deissmann, such a comparison was inappropriate, for Paul did not write artistic prose. He argued that one should keep in mind the contrast between artless, nonliterary prose, like Paul's, and artistic prose, which followed the canons of rhetorical theory.[69] Paul was a man of the people, and his letters show none of the artificiality of the sophists.

Until recently, Paul's rhetoric had not been the object of extensive study.[70] Judge himself has now studied contemporary professional practice in light of Paul's disavowal of rhetorical finesse and has concluded that Paul could not have been trained in it. Paul was a reluctant and unwelcomed competitor in the field of professional sophistry. The problem of defining Paul's rhetoric still remains, but Judge thinks that he can already draw sociological conclusions from the fact that Paul did practice the art: "Because it was learned only at the tertiary stage of education it formed a peculiarly conspicuous social dividing line between those who belonged to the leisured circles for whom such education was possible and those who could only afford the common literacy necessary to earning one's living. It

68. *Cf.*, Norden, *Die antike Kunstprosa*, II, 492ff.; Paul Wendland, *Die urchristlichen Literaturformen* (Tübingen, Germany, 1912), 353ff. Both, however, recognized the originality of Paul's style but believed that it did not measure up to the standards of artistic prose. Unfortunately, neither took up the invitation of J. Weiss to experts in ancient rhetoric to relate his analysis of some aspects of Paul's style to rhetorical practice. *Cf.*, Johannes Weiss, "Beiträge zur paulinischen Rhetorik," in *Theologische Studien: Festschrift Bernhard Weiss* (Göttingen, Germany, 1897), 165–247.

69. Deissmann, *Light from the Ancient East*, 3f., 69f. See also his review of Weiss's and Norden's works in *Theologische Rundschau*, V (1902), 65ff., where he expresses his uneasiness even about speaking of a Pauline "rhetoric," which suggests to him something too studied to be applied to Paul.

70. *Cf.*, Norbert Schneider, *Die rhetorische Eigenart der paulinischen Antithese* (Tübingen, Germany, 1970), for a renewed, but heavy, theological interest.

is important to grasp the importance of this boundary, for Paul, whose calling set him in close relations with those who were established above it, made it his peculiar boast (surely rhetorical) that he fell below it in both respects. He could not speak, and he had to work." [71]

One may not agree entirely with Judge. For example, it is not certain that rhetoric was learned only in the third educational stage. In the Greco-Roman period, training in rhetoric had been annexed to some degree by teachers in the secondary schools. [72] Furthermore, if Paul could have acquired the art without having been formally schooled in it, as Judge argues, then perhaps rhetorical facility did not form a conspicuous social dividing line. [73] To stress that it did negates the fact that only a minority in the churches may have belonged to that class. And whether tradesmen and artisans can rightly be called "leisured" is surely to be questioned.

We should also be careful not to presume, on the basis of Paul's rhetoric, the level of rhetorical sophistication of the churches to which he wrote. We should at least consider the possibility that Paul's rhetorical or literary ability distinguished him from most of his converts. [74] At most, rhetorical ability or

71. E. A. Judge, "Paul's Boasting in Relation to Contemporary Professional Practice," *Australian Biblical Review*, XVI (1968), 44.

72. *Cf.*, Marrou, *A History of Education in Antiquity*, 233ff. Note also that Martin P. Nilsson, *Die hellenistische Schule*, modifies Marrou's assignment of subject matter studied in the three stages of the educational process still further. Many of the inscriptions that Marrou believes refer to the third phase, after the age of eighteen, Nilsson considers to belong to secondary education, or to youths fifteen to eighteen years old.

73. The evidence advanced by G. W. Bowersock, *Greek Sophists in the Roman Empire* (Oxford, 1969), 21f., which shows that sophists generally did not come from the low or middle classes, does not apply to Paul. Bowersock deals with the second century, and with a class of sophists whose concerns and social roles were totally different from those of Paul.

74. Wendland, *Die urchristlichen Literaturformen*, 353, suggests that this was the case, and Werner Straub, *Die Bildersprache des Apostels Paulus* (Tübingen, Germany, 1937), 11f., claims to find evidence that the uneducated recipients of Paul's letters had difficulty in understanding them.

interest in the practice may be taken as part of the cumulative evidence showing that the Pauline churches included some educated people. What is more significant than its indication of social level is what it tells us of the educational, theological, and social values of some members of the Corinthian church, who expressed those values in their high appreciation of the art of persuasion.

The literary character of Paul's letters forms one aspect of the question of his literary and rhetorical culture. As we have noted, Deissmann believed that the newly discovered papyrus letters represented the literary culture of the common people and contributed by far the most important parallels to Paul's letters. His insistence that Paul's letters are "real letters" rather than "epistles," which were literary productions, is very well known. Deissmann's definition met with immediate criticism, but his understanding of Paul's letters has, in general, become the accepted one.[75] It may not be fair to say that epistolographic research has been somewhat stagnant since Deissmann,[76] but his concentration on the papyri has influenced form criticism studies of letters until recently.[77]

Deissmann found Franz Overbeck's opinion, that Paul's letters could not properly be classed as literature, stimulating. Overbeck justified his claim by arguing that Paul's written words were nothing other than an artless and casual surrogate for what Paul would have said had he been present with his

75. Deissmann, *Light from the Ancient East*, 146ff. *Cf.*, John C. Hurd, *The Origin of I Corinthians* (London, 1965), 3f.

76. See Judge, "St. Paul and Classical Society," 33 *n.* 75.

77. See Beda Rigaux, *The Letters of St. Paul: Modern Studies*, ed. and trans. S. Yonick (Chicago, 1968), Chap. 6. See also John L. White, *The Form and Function of the Body of the Greek Letter* (Missoula, Mont., 1972); White's *The Form and Structure of the Official Petition* (Missoula, Mont.: 1972), and Chan-Hie Kim, *Form and Structure of the Familiar Greek Letter of Recommendation* (Missoula, Mont., 1972). For a broader survey, see William G. Doty, *Letters in Primitive Christianity* (Philadelphia, 1973). Occasionally nonpapyrus materials were brought into the discussion, as in Carl J. Bjerkelund, *Parakalo* (Oslo, 1967); but generally, interest has been focused on the papyrus letters.

readers.[78] Eduard Norden partially agreed with Overbeck but cautioned that the letter had gradually become an accepted literary form. He then demonstrated that, when not measured by the standards of classical rhetoric, Paul appears as a stylist of some consequence.[79] Norden is surely correct, but what is needed is not simply further investigation into Paul's style in light of the rhetorical theory and practice of his time, but an examination of his letters in light of the epistolary theory and practice of his time. Ancient writers had an interest in what constituted the proper subject matter and style of a letter, and Paul's letters will be illuminated by their prescriptions for letter writing as well as by the letters of men who were familiar with the theory. It is ironic that Overbeck's description of Paul's letters is almost exactly the definition of a letter given by the handbooks on letter writing.[80]

Work done recently by members of the Society of Biblical Literature's seminar on "The Form and Function of the Pauline Letters" has reflected a desire to take into consideration epistolographic materials excluded or neglected by Deissmann and most of his followers. Sensitivity to the classifications of letters provided by ancient handbooks on letter writing, and utilization of "literary" letters, especially those of Cicero and Seneca, as well as the work of ancient rhetorical theorists, have contributed to a different perspective on Paul's letters.[81]

78. Deissmann, *Light from the Ancient East*, 147, on Franz Overbeck, "Über die Anfänge der patristischen Literatur," *Historische Zeitschrift*, XII (1882), esp. 429. The same view is still reflected by Wolfgang Wiefel, "Der Wandlung der Formen in der früchristlichen Literatur als soziologisches Problem," in *VIᵉ Conférence Internationale d'Études Classiques des Pays Socialistes* (Academia Scientarum Bulgarica. Acta Antiqua Philippopolitana. Studia Historica et Philologica.) (Sofia, Bulgaria, 1963), 319ff.

79. Norden, *Die Antike Kunstprosa*, II, 492ff.

80. For example, ps. Demetrius *Typoi Epistolikoi*, p. 2, l. 19ff. and ps. Proclus *Peri Epistolimaiou Characteros*, p. 27, l. 10, in the Weichert edition.

81. For example, Abraham J. Malherbe, "I Thessalonians as a Paraenetic Letter" (Paper delivered at the 1972 SBL Seminar on the Form and Function of the

The primary importance of this approach to the study of Paul's letters is not the contribution that it makes to our understanding of the social level of Paul and his churches. What it does demonstrate is that a wider range of possibilities is open to us in our attempts to understand Paul more fully. However, it is likely that further investigation of Paul's style of letter writing will further modify Deissmann's view of the social level represented by Paul's letters. It may be significant, for example, that letters were written as an exercise in style early in the tertiary stage of the educational system.[82] If Paul's letters can be shown to reflect the stylistic conventions associated with instruction on that level,[83] we would have one more piece of evidence that shows that Deissmann aimed too low.

Pauline Letters), incorporated in "Hellenistic Moralists and the New Testament"; Nils A. Dahl, "Paul's Letter to the Galatians: Epistolary Genre, Content, and Structure" (Paper delivered at the 1973 SBL Seminar); and the following papers discussed at the 1974 SBL Seminar: Robin Scroggs, "Paul as Rhetorician: Two Homilies in Romans 1–11"; Wilhelm Wuellner, "Digression in I Corinthians: The Rhetoric of Argumentation in Paul," and Hans Dieter Betz, "The Literary Composition and Function of Paul's Letter to the Galatians," the latter published in *New Testament Studies*, XXI (1975), 353–79. See also Betz's study of II Corinthians 10–13, *Der Apostel Paulus und die sokratische Tradition* (Tübingen, Germany, 1972).

82. See the introduction to Abraham J. Malherbe, *Ancient Epistolary Theorists* (Missoula, Mont., 1977).

83. Betz's studies (*n.* 81 above) presuppose a level of knowledge at least as high as that gained in the tertiary stage. Note also the references by Hans Windisch, *Der zweite Korintherbrief* (Göttingen, Germany, 1924), 75, 82, 84, 211, 221, 230, 414, to the correspondences with instructions in the handbooks; he does not, however, discuss them in any depth.

3

House Churches and Their Problems

THE CURRENT interest in the social aspect of early Christianity has called for attention to be focused on the communities formed by Christians. Several difficulties, however, confront us in our attempts to describe their constitution from within. I have tried to identify some of those problems and have concentrated on one interpretation of early Christian groups that regards them as scholastic communities. However, it is also desirable to know the physical and sociological circumstances of early Christian communal life and to ascertain whether and how those circumstances affected that life.

We may compare the early churches, or at least some aspects of them, to other ancient groups and have our understanding of them sharpened. But we run the risk of interpreting and reinterpreting Christian communities on analogy to one ancient group after another while never really understanding the Christian groups from within. It is necessary to begin with the information provided by the New Testament itself, and I suggest that an investigation of the Christian house churches will be a fruitful beginning.

Floyd Filson has pointed out five ways that a study of the house church furthers our understanding of the apostolic church: 1) Although Christian worship was indebted to Jewish practices, the house church made possible "a distinctly Christian worship and fellowship from the very first days of the apostolic age"; 2) the house churches make intelligible "the great attention paid to family life in the letters of Paul and in other Christian writings"; 3) the "existence of several house churches in one city goes far to explain the tendency to party strife in the apostolic age"; 4) "a study of the house church situation also throws light upon the social status of early Christians. . . . The apostolic church was more nearly a cross section of society than we have sometimes thought"; 5) "the development of church polity can never be understood without reference to the house churches. . . . The house church was the training ground for the Christian leaders who were to build the church after the loss of 'apostolic' guidance, and everything in such a situation favored the emergence of the host as the most prominent and influential member of the group. The strong leader of one such group might assume leadership throughout a city or section, although, as 3 John may suggest, such a development would not as a rule be free from friction." [1]

Although no major work has been devoted to the New Testament house church, recent studies have demonstrated the way in which an awareness of the phenomenon aids our understanding of certain New Testament texts. [2]

1. Floyd Filson, "The Significance of the Early House Churches," *Journal of Biblical Literature*, LVIII (1939), 109–12.

2. In addition to the literature cited below, see *Theological Dictionary of the New Testament*, s.v. "oikos"; E. A. Judge, *The Social Pattern of Christian Groups in the First Century* (London, 1960), Chap. 6; Willy Rordorff, "Was wissen wir über die christlichen Gottesdiensträume?" *Zeitschrift für die neutestamentliche Wissenschaft*, LV (1964), 110–28; Michael Green, *Evangelism in the Early Church* (London, 1970), 81, 207–23, 326; N. Afanasieff, "L'assemblée eucharistique unique dans l'église ancienne," *Kleronomia*, VI (1974), 1–36.

I

Before turning to the house church, we should have some understanding of the way early Christianity spread. Adolf Harnack influenced both scholarly and popular opinion in his magisterial work, which provided a brief sketch of the external conditions of the worldwide expansion of Christianity.[3] Reflecting popular opinion, Roland Allen thinks that Paul envisioned Roman provinces rather than cities as his fields of labor. The cities or towns in which he established churches "were centers of Roman administration, of Greek civilization, of Jewish influence, or of some commercial importance."[4] Although Allen, following Harnack, does mention that these cities were on the great highways of the Empire, his view of Christianity's spread is that of a series of concentric circles with the first church in a province at the center. That is part of the story, but it does not do justice to the importance of the mobility of Roman society as a major factor in determining the spread and social character of early Christianity.

The spread of Greek culture and language, Roman road-building and political administration, and the security brought about by the Roman army all contributed to the comparative ease of travel. The impression gained from such writers as Horace is that traveling was not very popular,[5] but the facts belie that notion. "It is the simple truth that travelling, whether for business or pleasure, was contemplated and performed under the Empire with an indifference, confidence, and, above all, certainty, which were unknown in after centuries until

3. Adolf von Harnack, *The Mission and Expansion of Christianity in the First Three Centuries*, trans. and ed. James Moffatt (2 vols.; New York, 1908), I, 19–23.
4. Roland Allen, *Missionary Methods: St. Paul's or Ours?* (6th ed.; Grand Rapids, Mich., 1962), 13. On a scholarly level, see Karl Holl, "Die Missionsmethode der alten und die mittelalterlichen Kirche," *Gesammelte Aufsätze* (3 vols.; Tübingen, Germany, 1928), III, 118f., for a similar view.
5. For example, Horace *Satire* I, v.

the introduction of steamers and the consequent increase in ease and sureness of communication." [6] Perhaps no one traveled as much as a certain Phrygian merchant whose tomb inscription claimed that in the course of his life he had traveled to Rome seventy-two times. But travel was, nevertheless, within the reach of many and was especially common among merchants and artisans. [7]

The churches we read about in the New Testament were established in important cities on the major trade routes. By the end of the first century, Christianity began spreading into the villages. But earliest Christianity was an urban phenomenon with all the problems, tensions, and possibilities which that implied, for in the cities, there was greater openness and a willingness to give a hearing to preachers of new religions. [8] Much remains to be done in working out the points of contact between the church and urban society as reflected in the New Testament. [9]

6. William M. Ramsay, "Roads and Travel in the New Testament," *Hastings Dictionary of the Bible*, V, 396. See also, Lionel Casson, *Travel in the Ancient World* (Toronto, 1974); G. Radke, "Viae Publicae Romanae," Pauly-Wissowa, *Realenzyklopädie*, Supplementary Vol. XIII (1973), 1417–86; Heinz E. Herzig, "Probleme des römischen Strassenwesens: Untersuchungen zur Geschichte und Recht," in Hildegard Temporini (ed.), *Aufstieg und Niedergang der römischen Welt* (7 vols. to date; Berlin, 1974—), Vol. II, Pt. 1, pp. 593–648.

7. G. LaFaye (ed.), *Inscriptiones Graecae ad res Romanas pertinentes* (4 vols.; Paris, 1927), IV, 290–91, No. 841.

8. A. D. Nock's description of how ancient cults spread in *Conversion* (Oxford, 1933), 48–98, presupposes the mobility of society. For the expansion of Christianity into the countryside by the second century, see Pliny *Epistle* X, 96; *cf.*, Justin Martyr *Apology* 67:3. *Cf.*, Einar Molland, "Besass die Alte Kirche ein Missionsprogramm und bewisste Missionsmethoden?" in *Die Alte Kirche* (Munich, 1974), 52f., Vol. I of Heinzgünter Frohnes and Uwe V. Knorr (eds.), *Kirchengeschichte als Missionsgeschichte* (Munich, 1974), and A. Kehl, "Antike Volksfrömmigkeit und das Christentum," in the same volume, 314f.

9. For conditions in the cities, see Ramsay MacMullen, *Enemies of the Roman Order: Treason, Unrest, Alienation in the Empire* (Cambridge, Mass., 1966), esp. Chap. 5, and his *Roman Social Relations 50 B.C. to A.D. 284* (New Haven, Conn., 1974), Chaps. 2 and 3. *Cf.*, E. A. Judge, "St. Paul and Classical Society," *Jahrbuch für Antike und Christentum*, XV (1972), 27.

Here I wish to stress that early Christianity shared in the mobility of its society. The preachers were themselves transient. Luke's understanding is that Paul generally spent only a few weeks or months with his newly established churches. The only exceptions are his stays in Corinth and Ephesus, where he remained for periods of eighteen months and three years.[10] Rather than preaching in the marketplaces in these cities, as other religious and philosophical preachers usually did, he seemed to prefer the synagogues. There he would come in contact with the God-fearers or God-worshipers, that class of Gentiles who had been attracted to the synagogues without becoming proselytes.[11] His coworkers, too, were not characterized by their permanent location. Aquila and Priscilla, for example, are placed at various times in Pontus, Rome, Corinth, Ephesus, and again in Rome. A close reading of Paul's letters reveals constant traveling by his associates as they maintained the contact between him and his churches. Some of them were artisans—Aquila and Priscilla, for instance, were tentmakers like Paul himself. Lydia, the seller of purple, was from Thyatira in Asia Minor, but was converted by Paul in northern Greece.[12]

The most dramatic illustration of the mobility of early Christians comes from Paul's letter to the church in Rome, written before he had ever been to that city. In the letter he introduces himself and his gospel, as he makes plans to visit the Romans and then go on to Spain. In chapter sixteen he greets by name

10. Acts 18:11; 19:8, 10 (*cf.*, 20:31).
11. See Nock, *Conversion*, 191f. For the importance of the God-fearers for the Christian mission, see Henneke Gülzow, "Soziale Gegebenheiten der altkirchlichen Mission," in *Die Alte Kirche* (Munich, 1974), 194ff., Vol. I of Frohnes and Knorr (eds.), *Kirchengeschichte als Missionsgeschichte*.
12. Regarding Aquila and Priscilla, see Acts 18:1–3; I Cor. 16:19; Rom. 16:3f. On Lydia, see Acts 16:14. For more information on Paul's coworkers, see Gottfried Schille, *Die urchristliche Kollegialmission* (Zurich, 1967); Earle E. Ellis, "Paul and His Co-Workers," *New Testament Studies*, XVII (1971), 437–52.

twenty-six persons with whom he had previously worked.[13]
These people, for various reasons, had found their way from
the eastern Mediterranean to Rome.

It was this mobility of the early church that was responsible
for the spread of the faith. Despite his concentration on his
heroes Peter and Paul, Luke reflects the view that not only
major figures took the gospel abroad.[14] This fact must be ap-
preciated if we are to have a proper perspective on early Christian communities. Contemporary New Testament scholarship
has recognized the importance of wandering preachers who
challenged Paul's congregations after he had left them. However, the stress on these opponents of Paul tends to diminish
the effect that the many other traveling Christians must have
had on the life of the church. Surely they did not create one
crisis after another, and they must have contributed to the formation of a network by which information about churches was
communicated. In this way they would have contributed to the
unity of the church and to whatever continuities characterized
early Christianity.[15] We happen to know more about the con-
troversies because that is where the heat was generated. Travel
caused confrontations between Christians of different viewpoints, and we are the richer for them because they make us
aware of the diversity that characterized early Christianity.
But it is doubtful that a realistic view of the church and its
faith can be obtained if the continuities are not also taken into
consideration.

The mobility of Roman society required provision for the
lodging and entertainment of travelers. This was done by inns,

13. For a convincing argument that Romans 16 was part of the original letter to
Rome, see Harry Y. Gamble, "The Textual History of the Letter to the Romans"
(Ph.D. Dissertation, Yale University, 1971).

14. Acts 8:4; 11:19ff.; 18:2(?), 24ff.; 28:13ff.

15. For the continuity in early Christianity, see Robert M. Grant, *Augustus to
Constantine* (New York, 1970), 251–312.

which were built in the cities and along the highways. The inns, however, were regarded as barely adequate and were avoided whenever possible by the upper classes. Innkeepers were frequently associated with magical practices, and it was commonly assumed that a traveler could obtain "commercial" female companionship in the inns. Therefore this institutionalized form of hospitality, widespread as it was, did not completely take the place of private hospitality, which had been regarded as a virtue since classical times by pagans as well as Jews.[16]

Jews, for obvious reasons, avoided the inns, choosing to care for their wandering brethren themselves. Christians appear to have followed their example. Luke, especially, shows an interest in hospitality and in its implications.[17] In his Gospel he frequently introduces material unique to him that places Jesus in a setting where hospitality is enjoyed and becomes part of Jesus' teaching (e.g., 14:7–14). In Acts of the Apostles, after the conversion of Cornelius the God-fearer, the controversy between Peter and the circumcision party revolves, not around Cornelius' baptism, but around Peter's eating with him (11:1ff.). Luke writes that, after her baptism, Lydia, another God-fearer, confronts Paul with a test of the validity of his preaching: "If you have judged me to be faithful to the Lord, come to my house and stay." And he adds, "And she prevailed upon us!"

16. On the inns, see Tönnes Kleberg, *Hôtels, restaurants et cabarets dans l'antiquité romaine* (Uppsala, Sweden, 1957), and Casson, *Travel in the Ancient World*, 197–218. On hospitality, see *Theological Dictionary of the New Testament*, s.v. "xenos"; Helga Rusche, *Gastfreundschaft in der Verkündigung des neuen Testaments und ihr Verhältnis zur Mission* (Münster, W. Germany, 1957), and John B. Mathews, "Hospitality and the New Testament Church: An Historical and Exegetical Study" (Th.D. Dissertation, Princeton Theological Seminary, 1965).

17. See Henry J. Cadbury, "Lexical Notes on Luke-Acts," *Journal of Biblical Literature*, XLV (1926), 305–22, and his *The Making of Luke-Acts* (London, 1958), 251ff.

(16:15). Luke clearly sees a theological significance in the practice.[18]

The Christian practice of hospitality was not viewed simply as a means of overcoming a practical problem. Theological statements by different authors in the New Testament show that it was frequently viewed as the concrete expression of Christian love. "Let love be genuine . . . love one another with brotherly affection . . . contribute to the needs of the saints, practice hospitality" (Rom. 13:9–13). "Let brotherly love continue. Do not neglect to show hospitality to strangers, for thereby some have entertained angels unawares" (Heb. 13:1–2). "Above all hold unfailing your love for one another, since love covers a multitude of sins. Practice hospitality ungrudgingly to one another. As each has received a gift, employ it for one another, as good stewards of God's varied grace" (I Pet. 4:8–10). The practice of early Christian hospitality has received some attention in the last decade, but its theological implications as perceived by the early church still await serious attention.

Traveling Christians appear to have assumed that they would be received hospitably wherever they went. This idea emerges

18. Luke is impressed by the social standing of the converted God-fearers (cf., Acts 17:4, 12; 18:7; cf., Luke 7:1–10); but as his accounts of the conversion of Cornelius and Lydia show, the sociological as well the theological implications of conversion are important to him. Jews had an ambivalent attitude toward proselytes and God-fearers. Despite the degrees to which these people adopted Judaism, social inequality between them and the Jews seemed to remain a fact of life. See George Foot Moore, *Judaism in the First Centuries of the Christian Era* (3 vols.; Cambridge, Mass., 1927), I, 335, 341ff.; *Theological Dictionary of the New Testament, s.v. "proselytos"*; K. G. Kuhn and H. Stegemann, "Proselyten," in Pauly-Wissowa, *Realenzyklopädie*, Supplementary Vol. IX, (1962), 1273ff. Luke, correctly reflecting current conditions, is in fact making the claim that such social inequality as existed between Jews and God-fearers for theological reasons did not exist in the church. Gülzow, "Soziale Gegebenheiten," 197, draws further attention to the social standing of the God-fearers as a factor which insured from the beginning that Christianity would not be a religion of the lower classes, but would be socially diverse.

from New Testament writings, especially Luke's (*e.g.*, Acts 21:4ff., 7f., 15f.). Using a vocabulary that had virtually become technical, travelers confidently planned their own and their companions' journeys on that assumption.[19] Paul writes to his friend Philemon to prepare a guest room for him (Philem. 22). He also expects his churches to bear the expenses for his trips. This is the connotation of *propempo*, translated "to speed on a journey." The term is used only in connection with traveling Christians in the New Testament, apparently in the sense of Titus 3:13f.: "Do your best to speed Zenas the lawyer and Apollos on their way; see that they lack nothing. And let our people learn to apply themselves to good deeds, so as to help cases of urgent need, and not to be unfruitful." In I Corinthians 16:6f., Paul tells that troublesome church: "I will visit you in passing through Macedonia, for I intend to pass through Macedonia, and perhaps I will stay with you or even pass the winter, so that you may speed me on my journey, wherever I go." Even to the church in Rome, which he had not established, he writes, "Since I have longed for many years to come to you, I hope to see you in passing as I go to Spain, and to be sped on my journey by you, once I have enjoyed your company for a little" (Rom. 15:23f.). It was not only Paul the Apostle who could expect hospitality; he also claimed it for his coworkers (*cf.*, I Cor. 16:11). At the end of the first century, traveling Christians still availed themselves of the hospitality of their brethren (*cf.*, III John).

The expression of hospitality that particularly concerns us here is the house church. The early church did not own buildings specially constructed for its religious activities. It met primarily in the homes of some of its members. Paul's missionary practice was to convert entire households after his ejection

---

19. *Cf.*, Mathews, "Hospitality and the New Testament Church," 166–74.

from the synagogues and then to use these houses as the bases for his further activity. From his letters it appears that his churches continued to meet in the homes of some of its members.[20] This fact is significant because in New Testament times the household was regarded as a basic political unit. In addition to members of the immediate family, slaves, freedmen, servants, laborers, and sometimes business associates and tenants were included. The household members' loyalty to the interests of the household was so strong that it could rival loyalty to the republic. The closeness of the household unit offered the security and sense of belonging not provided by larger political and social structures. The head of the household had a degree of legal responsibility for his charges, but the solidarity of the group was based more on economic, and especially psychological, social, and religious factors.[21]

Converts would join themselves to a household church during its earliest period of growth in a particular locality. The household character of a church would be retained as it became a community with a broader constituency than it originally had. The converts also had demands placed upon them, which heightened the exclusiveness of the group. When they spoke of "outsiders," early Christians revealed their minority group mind-set. They believed that they had been called to a higher quality of life than could be expected of their society, and they took measures to safeguard it through their communities. The implications of the preaching that called the communities into existence had to be worked out by those commu-

20. Acts 16:15, 31ff.; 17:6; 18:1–8; Rom. 16:3ff.; I Cor. 1:14–16; 16:19; Philem. 2.
21. See Judge, *The Social Pattern of Christian Groups*, Chap. 3; August Strobel, "Der Begriff des 'Hauses' im griechischen und römischen Privatrecht," *Zeitschrift für die neutestamentliche Wissenschaft*, LVI (1965), 91–100; J. Gaudemet, "Familie I (Familienrecht)," *Reallexikon für Antike und Christentum* (1969), VII, 331ff.; Gülzow, "Soziale Gegebenheiten," 192f., 198f.

nities, which were private, voluntary organizations. This means that early Christians did not see themselves as isolated individuals; and the nature of those communities becomes clearer to us when we see them as household communities. It is striking how often the New Testament deals with issues in relation to the Christian community.

As the church grew in a particular locality, more than one house church would be formed.[22] The scarcity of information on the house churches in the first century precludes our having a clear understanding of their interrelationship. Paul seems to have known of at least three such churches in Rome (Rom. 16:5, 14, 15), and there may have been more than one group in Thessalonica (I Thess. 5:27) and also in Laodicea (Col. 4:15). Although they may have formed separate communities, such groups were not viewed as being separate churches. Luke's description of the church in Jerusalem is not clear on this point, but it does convey the impression that he thought of it as one church despite the smaller groups that composed it. This is supported by his (and the Pastoral Epistles') relating presbyters, or bishops, to cities rather than to individual groups (Acts 14:23; 20:17; Titus 1:5). By that time, however, more than one house church would presumably have existed in most localities with which the literature is concerned. More significant is that Paul and his followers, although they knew of separate groups in an area, wrote one letter to the church in that immediate area, apparently on the assumption that it would suffice for all the groups (*e.g.*, Romans). On this understanding, the individual house churches would together have represented the church in any one area.

22. For greater detail, see Abraham J. Malherbe, "The Inhospitality of Diotrephes," in the Festschrift for Nils Dahl, edited by Jacob Jervell and Wayne A. Meeks, *God's Christ and His People* (Oslo, 1976).

II

Gerd Theissen has recently published a series of impressive articles on some of the results of his sociological study of early Christianity.[23] In three of the articles he is concerned primarily with the church in Corinth.[24] Theissen's thesis is that the church in Corinth was characterized by an inner social stratification that was responsible for much of the tension in its communal life.[25]

He begins by painstakingly evaluating statements on the Corinthian church as a whole that may cast light on its social constituency. The principal text he uses is I Corinthians 1:26–29: "For consider your call brethren; not many of you were wise according to worldly standards, not many were powerful, not many were of noble birth [*eugeneis*]; but God chose what is foolish in the world to shame the wise, God chose what is weak in the world to shame the strong, God chose what is lowly [*ta agene*] and despised in the world [*ta exouthenemena*], even things that are not [*ta me onta*] to bring to nothing things that are, so that no human being might boast in the presence of God." Of the three categories of people Paul mentions—the

23. Gerd Theissen, "Wanderradikalismus: Literarsoziologische Aspekte von Worten Jesu im Urchristentum," *Zeitschrift für Theologie und Kirche*, LXX (1973), 245–71; and "Theoretische Probleme religionssoziologischer Forschung und die Analyse des Urchristentums," *Neue Zeitschrift für systematische Theologie und Religionsphilosophie*, XVI (1974), 35–56.

24. Gerd Theissen, "Legitimation und Lebensunterhalt: Ein Beitrag zur Soziologie urchristlicher Missionäre," *New Testament Studies*, XXI (1975), 192–221, also deals with Corinth, but is not considered here.

25. Gerd Theissen, "Soziale Schichtung in der korinthischen Gemeinde: Ein Beitrag zur Soziologie des hellenistischen Urchristentums," *Zeitschrift für die neutestamentliche Wissenschaft*, LXV (1974), 232–72. Theissen claims that his findings apply, *mutatis mutandis*, to other Hellenistic Pauline churches. The early Palestinian Christian movement is considered to have been rural in character (p. 269), *cf.*, Theissen's "Legitimation und Lebensunterhalt," 196f., 200ff.; and see M. Hengel, "Zwischen Jesus und Paulus: Die 'Hellenisten,' die 'Sieben' und Stephanus," *Zeitschrift für Theologie und Kirche*, LXXII (1975), esp. 200, for the importance of the Hellenists (Acts 6, 7) in making Christianity a religion of the cities. See further, Judge, *The Social Pattern of Christian Groups*, 7–17.

wise, the powerful, and those of noble birth—the last is a specifically sociological category. Paul stresses this further by not
merely contrasting noble birth with lowly birth, but by using
the terms *ta exouthenemena* and *ta me onta*, which were commonly used to describe people of lower rank. This suggests
that the first two categories are also to be understood in a sociological sense; that is, they describe men whose wisdom was a
sign of their social status and who were socially influential.

When Paul says that not many of the Corinthian Christians
were from the upper social strata, he assumes that some, at
least, were. Although they may only have been a minority,
they were a dominating minority. Much of I Corinthians is
written with them in mind, and in his admonitions Paul no-
ticeably tends to rank himself with those of lesser means. The
social stratification of the church becomes clearer when one
examines what is said about its individual members with respect to their position or occupations, their households, the
services they provided for the church, and their travels.

Crispus, one of the few Christians whom Paul had personally baptized in Corinth, was a ruler of the synagogue (Acts
18:8; I Cor. 1:14). Men occupying that position were persons
of private means, for the cost of the upkeep, and occasionally
even the building of a synagogue, could fall to them. Therefore
they were highly respected by the Jewish community. Some
tomb inscriptions suggest that they were highly regarded by
people outside the Jewish community, but the evidence for
that is less sure.

Paul mentions that Erastus was city treasurer (Rom. 16:23).
The exact contemporary meaning of the term applied to Erastus, *ho oikonomos tes poleos*, has been hotly disputed. Some
have argued that it designated a high city official, and others, a
minor financial officer, possibly a slave owned by the city. After an exhaustive study of the evidence, Theissen concludes

that Erastus was a Roman citizen, possibly a freedman, and a man of some personal wealth.

Two Corinthians were said to be converted with their households: Crispus (Acts 18:8) and Stephanas (I Cor. 1:16; *cf.*, 16:14ff.). Theissen notes that the passages relating to them provide information about their personal circumstances rather than their social status. These writings must be taken in conjunction with the other evidence. Nevertheless, Theissen points out that Luke's four accounts of household conversion involve people who were part of the "establishment" (a centurion, a tradeswoman, a civil servant, and a ruler of a synagogue). [26] Their households could be expected to have included slaves and servants. From this he infers that the mention of households suggests that their heads were persons of means, thus including Stephanas the Corinthian. [27]

Of the services rendered the congregation, that of providing quarters for the church's meeting is of major importance. When Paul wrote Romans while he was in Corinth, Gaius was host to him as well as to the whole church (Rom. 16:23). According to Acts 18:10, and judging from the number of Corinthians whom we know by name, the church in Corinth must have been quite large, and Gaius' house must therefore have

---

26. Acts 10:1ff.; 16:14ff., 32ff.; 18:8ff.

27. I must demur to Theissen's method of arguing at this point. He uses Acts to a striking degree to complement information from Paul's letters in his description of the church in Corinth. It must be granted that, despite widespread skepticism of the historical reliability of Acts, the situation regarding its information on Corinth is different. Günther Bornkamm, *Paul*, trans. D. M. G. Stalker (New York, 1969), 68, reflects critical opinion: "The account in Acts furnishes reliable, detailed information about which there is no dispute (18:1–17)." But Theissen's attempt to prove that Stephanas was a man of means is not convincing. We know Stephanas only from Paul's casual references in I Corinthians 1:16 and 16:15ff. To regard him as a person of means on the basis of Luke's description of other individuals, is methodologically unjustified, especially since Luke's descriptions reflect his tendency to present Christians as people of some social status. Perhaps the fact that Stephanas traveled to see Paul (I Cor. 16:17) may point in that direction, but not even that is certain.

been quite spacious to accommodate them all.[28] Also, at the very end of the letter Gaius is mentioned in company with Tertius the stenographer and Erastus the city treasurer, people who might have been closely associated with him. Tertius may have been a slave amanuensis, but Theissen argues that it is equally possible that he was employed by the provincial administration. The point is that we should visualize a large church in Corinth meeting in the home of a wealthy patron whose associates, of equal social status, are also members of the church.

At the beginning of his mission in Corinth Paul had stayed with Aquila and Priscilla, who were, like himself, tentmakers (Acts 18:3) who followed their trade from place to place. That they were of more than moderate means may be indicated by the fact that they had a church meeting in their house in Ephesus.[29] After Silas and Timothy arrived with financial aid from Macedonia, Paul transferred his activities to the house of Titius Justus, a God-fearer who lived next door to the synagogue.[30] We do not know why Paul made the change, but the

28. It is possible that Paul means that Gaius extended hospitality to all other Christian travelers as he did to Paul, and not that all the Christians in the city habitually met in his house. Cf., M. J. Lagrange, *Épitre aux Romains* (Paris, 1950), on Romans 16:23. However, Paul's mention of the church in the house of Priscilla and Aquila in 16:5, and his possible reference to two other house churches in 16:14, 15, may suggest that the Corinthian church met in Gaius' house. If this were the case, the situation in Corinth may have been different from other areas, where a number of house churches would soon have been formed. See Malherbe, "The Inhospitality of Diotrephes."

29. I Cor. 16:19; Rom. 16:3. Theissen assumes, with most scholars, that Romans 16 was addressed to Ephesus, but see *n.* 13 above.

30. Theissen assumes, as Codex Bezae does, that Acts 18:7 describes Paul's removal from the house of Aquila to that of Titius Justus. The reason suggested is the more favorable location of the latter. But there is no evidence in the text to support the opinion. Luke is describing the changes in location of Paul's preaching activity, not of his lodging. While living with Priscilla and Aquila and supporting himself, he preached in the synagogue only on the sabbath (Acts 18:4). When Silas and Timothy arrived, probably with financial aid from Macedonia (Acts 18:5; *cf.*, II Cor. 11:9;

context in Acts suggests that the location of Titius Justus' house next door to the synagogue was important to Paul. It is interesting to us that, although archaeologists have not found the synagogue, an inscription entitled "synagogue of the Hebrews" has been found in the neighborhood of the agora, the area where small shops of artisans were located.[31] Paul, therefore, seems to have concentrated his work in Corinth among people of the artisan and merchant classes. These indications of wealth and social status assume greater value when they are seen in conjunction with the statements about the travels of the Corinthians.

The ability to travel was not characteristic only of the well-to-do, and by itself does not necessarily signify the economic or social status of the Corinthians. Again we point to the cumulative nature of the evidence. We know seventeen persons and groups of persons by name, nine of whom we meet on travels. It is quite likely, in view of other evidence, that their reasons for traveling were commercial. Theissen points out that most of the people named are of comparatively high social status. They would naturally exert influence in the congregation and would be enabled by their mobility to keep up communication with Paul. He concludes that the most active and important members of the congregation most probably belonged to the

---

Phil. 4:15?), he devoted all his time to preaching to the Jews, possibly with the synagogue as his base. When they rejected him, he changed his teaching locality to the house of Titius Justus (Acts 18:6f.). It is not clear whether Luke supposes that two groups of Christians were then meeting in Corinth, one each in the homes of Priscilla and Aquila, and Titius Justus. If there were two groups, and if we reconciled Acts with the interpretation of Romans 16:23 presented in *n.* 28 above, then the meeting of the entire church in the house of Gaius six years later would be the result of the consolidation of a number of groups. Given the transience of such hosts to the churches as Priscilla and Aquila, it must not have been unusual for churches to move from one house to another.

31. It may be possible to determine the location more precisely by following the method of MacMullen, *Roman Social Relations*, 69ff.

categories of the wise, the powerful, and the nobly born. The less favored members of the congregation are scarcely mentioned individually in the Corinthian correspondence. [32]

Comments made by Paul about parts of the congregation confirm what can be learned about individuals in the church. It can be argued that the Corinthians' attitude toward the support of missionaries confirms their financial status. They appear to have supported Peter, Apollos, and Paul's opponents, about whom we learn in II Corinthians. Part of the opponents' controversy with Paul was that he did not wish to receive support from the congregation. [33] Theissen supposes that such an attitude indicates that some of the Corinthians were well-off. This may not be entirely convincing, but it is clear that finances were important to the Corinthians. This is shown in Paul's discussions of his own support, of the collection for Jerusalem, and of his injunction that Christians should not go to court when defrauded by their brethren (I Cor. 6:1–11). The willingness of some Corinthians to go to court probably also reflects the confidence of socially well-established persons that they would receive justice from the legal system.

These findings agree with what we know of the social structure of Corinth. The Roman element was strong in this Greek city, and it is interesting that of the seventeen known names of Christians, eight are Latin names. Other cults besides the Jews were established there, the best known being that of Isis, which illustrates that the Corinthians were open to new religious traditions. The social mobility of Corinthian society further contributed to the heterogeneous character of the city. In addition, Corinth was a center of commerce, industry, and banking; the location of the Isthmian games; and the capital of

32. *Cf.*, Judge, pp. 29–30 herein.
33. I Cor. 9:1ff.; II Cor. 1–13. I Cor. 9:3; 16:2 may indicate differences in financial ability.

the province of Achaia. The social stratification of the city was known to be pronounced, with sharp contrasts between the rich and the poor. The Christian community, which included people from quite different social strata, might be expected to have particular problems with social integration.

In this light it is significant that Paul, although he knew that the majority of his converts came from among the poor, personally baptized only people from the higher strata, such as Crispus, Gaius, and Stephanas (I Cor. 1:14, 16). Theissen claims that they were more receptive to Paul's preaching, and for that he posits a sociological reason. Acts of the Apostles indicates that Paul met with particular success in preaching to the God-fearers, who were generally of higher social standing than proselytes. By adopting the worship of the Jewish God, they had already demonstrated their independence from their native religious traditions. Moreover, the preaching of Paul offered them a monotheism and high ethics without the Jewish restrictions of circumcision and ritual requirements.[34]

Sociological grounds for the conversion of such people may also be found with Paul himself and his method of missionizing. Paul came from the same social stratum as his earliest converts. He too was an artisan who traveled extensively, and he was a Roman citizen, a fact that conferred on him some privilege and perhaps dignity.[35] Paul lived with his social equals and used their homes as bases for his missionary operation. Nevertheless, the congregation in Corinth soon counted more members from the lower ranks than the upper. The social strata within the church were no longer simply derived from

34. *Cf.*, notes 11 and 18 above.
35. *Cf.*, Dio Chrysostom *Oration* 34:21–23, for the mistreatment of textile workers in Tarsus who, unlike Paul, were not citizens. On this passage, see further Hans Böhlig, *Die Geisteskultur von Tarsus im augusteischen Zeitalter* (Göttingen, Germany, 1913), 130ff.; MacMullen, *Roman Social Relations*, 59f., but see Judge, p. 47 *n.* 45 herein.

the extended household in which there were slaves and servants, but must have increased with the conversion of other persons of lesser means. "The interests brought together in this way probably marked the Christians off from the other unofficial associations, which were generally socially and economically as homogeneous as possible. Certainly the phenomenon led to constant differences among the Christians themselves."[36]

This social stratification of the Corinthian church, Theissen argues, was responsible for the tension between the "weak" and the "strong" Christians in Corinth over the question of eating meat offered to idols (I Cor. 8, 10).[37] He does not question the legitimacy of seeking for the theological grounds of the conflict, but he is convinced that sociological analysis is not thereby excluded and that such an analysis does not reduce a theological conflict to social factors. He insists, however, that, as a rule, theological convictions become operative only when social groups bestow on them the power to govern their conduct.

Theissen rejects attempts to identify the weak Christians as either Jews or Gentiles. He claims that Paul himself saw the problem as a general one[38] and that socioeconomic factors enable us to understand the situation. Paul had drawn a contrast between the weak and strong in I Corinthians 1:26ff. and had related that contrast to the social structure of the Corinthian

36. Quoted by Theissen, with approval, from Judge, *Social Pattern of Christian Groups*, 60. Theissen differs from Judge in that he does not believe the social stratification in the church simply reflects that of the converted households. Gülzow also argued that the social stratification of the church distinguished it from other associations, "Soziale Gegebenheiten," 190ff., 220f. See also *n*. 18 above.

37. Gerd Theissen, "Die Starken und Schwachen in Korinth: Soziologische Analyse eines theologischen Streites," *Evangelische Theologie*, XXXV (1975), 155–72.

38. Paul presents his own conduct as an example to both Jews and Gentiles (I Cor. 9:19–23), and his injunction not to give offense to Jews or Greeks (10:32) implies that the weak could be either. Furthermore, whereas 8:7 refers to Gentile Christians, 8:10 could refer to either.

church. The weak Christians, therefore, are to be found in the lower social strata rather than in a particular national group. And Paul identifies himself with them in his discussion of their problems.[39]

Theissen points out that the diet of the majority of the lower classes, from which most of the Corinthians came, included very little meat. The problem of eating meat sold in the market (I Cor. 10:25ff.) was to them purely theoretical, for they did not have the money to buy it. However, that is not the real problem, for Paul concerns himself mostly with the eating of meat at cultic meals within official settings. All inhabitants of cities, regardless of their social status, could eat meat during the public festivals and the cultic meals of the many popular associations and clubs. But Theissen questions whether members from the lower social strata always attended those meals that contained meat. The upshot is that, following their conversion to Christianity, the lower classes found it difficult to eat meat without recalling pagan religious festivals and idol worship and thus hurting their consciences (8:7). Converted Jews, liberated from the restrictions of Judaism, also found it difficult to deal with the public distribution of meat (8:10).[40]

39. Cf., I Cor. 4:10; 9:22.
40. Theissen, "Die Starken und Schwachen," is not clear about where the Gentile Christians would partake of meat. In one place (p. 162) he states that they must have been tempted not to forego meat available during the festivals and in the associations; but elsewhere (pp. 164f.) he expresses reservation on the latter possibility, because many of the associations may not have provided more elaborate meals than the bread and wine of the Lord's Supper. He also denies that the weak and the strong were together with pagans at meals where meat was served (I Cor. 10:27–30). He does not consider the implications of the position that practically all meat sold in the market came from animals ritually slaughtered. See Arnold Ehrhardt, "Social Problems in the Early Church," in his *The Framework of the New Testament Stories* (Cambridge, Mass., 1964), 280, and the reservation expressed by Hans Conzelmann, *I Corinthians*, trans. James W. Leitch (Philadelphia, 1975), 176. See further, *n.* 47 below. The problems of Jewish Christians do not seem to be clarified by considerations of social status, and Theissen does not elaborate on how their traditions influenced them in their new situation.

The strong Christians from the upper classes, however, were accustomed to eating meat daily and therefore did not associate it with a cult. Furthermore, the professional responsibilities of a man like Erastus, involving construction of public buildings and squares, required that he show a less reserved attitude toward "consecrated meat." [41] The continued contact of the strong Christians with pagans included their attendance at pagan banquets, where they would eat what was set before them without reservation (I Cor. 10:25–30). They justified their conduct by appealing to their "knowledge," thus revealing parallels with later Christian Gnostics, who also had a liberal attitude toward eating meat offered to idols. But Theissen does not suggest that there was a continuity between the Corinthian "gnosis" and the Christian Gnosticism of the second century. The analogy between the two is that in both, the Christian faith underwent a typical transformation as it rose in the higher social levels. Both have factors which can be explained by their comparable social situations—namely, the high intellectual level of their systems of thought, their trust in the saving power of knowledge, their elitism within the congregation, and their relative openness to the pagan world. [42] Theissen argues that Paul was informed of the conflict between the weak and the strong Christians in a letter that was

41. Theissen also draws the sociological conclusion from the way greed and idolatry are connected in paraenesis (Col. 3:6; Eph. 5:5; cf., I Cor. 5:10f.) that whoever wishes to be rich or is rich must cultivate contact with pagans. This conclusion must be rejected, not only on the grounds that the lists of vices derive from Hellenistic Judaism and are to be understood theologically rather than sociologically, but also because it is unrealistic to absolve the poor of greed!

42. Cf., H. G. Kippenberg, "Versuch einer soziologischen Verortung des antiken Gnostizismus," Numen, XVII (1970), 211–31, and the criticisms by P. Munz, "The Problem of 'Die soziologische Verortung des antiken Gnostizismus'," Numen, XIX (1972), 41–51. Theissen's differentiation of the Corinthians disagrees with the distinction between the nonintellectual early Christians and the later Gnostics, made by John G. Gager, Kingdom and Community: The Social World of Early Christianity (Englewood Cliffs, N.J., 1975), 5, 106f. Cf., p. 46n. 43 herein.

clearly written from the standpoint of the strong (*cf.*, I Cor. 8:1), but he also received oral information (*cf.*, I Cor. 1:11; 11:18) "from below" (*cf.*, I Cor. 1:26ff.; 11:20ff.).[43] Paul then addressed his reply almost exclusively to the strong.[44]

The weak and the strong Christians did eat the Lord's Supper together; and on those occasions, too, their different social levels were responsible for tensions. Theissen offers the hypothesis that the conflict described in I Corinthians 11 had social causes that become clearer when confronted with the theological arguments of 11:17ff.[45]

Theissen analyzes the most important statements in I Corinthians 11:17–34 to determine the problems. Paul charges the Corinthians with not in fact eating the Lord's Supper. "When you meet together, it is not the Lord's supper [*kuriakon deipnon*] that you eat. For in eating, each one goes ahead with his own meal [*idion deipnon*] and one is hungry and another is drunk. What! Do you not have houses to eat and drink in? Or do you despise the church of God and humiliate those who have nothing?" (11:20ff.). The conflict appears to be caused by excessive individualism, but in view of the divisions (*schismata*, 11:18) and factions (*haireseis*, 11:19) remarked by Paul, Theissen considers it more likely that he has two groups in mind—those who have their own meal and those who have nothing. The meal eaten by the wealthy is contrasted with the Lord's

43. To fit the oral report of "Chloe's people" (I Cor. 1:11) into his theory, Theissen suggests that they were from the lower classes—probably slaves or dependents of Chloe, although they traveled and thus met one of his criteria for belonging to the upper strata. See his "Soziale Schichtung," 253f., 255f.

44. Almost all passages written in the second person are addressed to them, *e.g.*, I Cor. 8:9, 10, 11; 10:15, 31. Paul's excursus in 9:1–27 considers two groups, those who criticize him for not accepting financial support (9:3), and the strong to whom he presents himself as an example. Theissen considers it likely that the two groups are the same.

45. Gerd Theissen, "Soziale Integration und sakramentale Handeln: Eine Analyse von I Kor. 11:17–34," *Novum Testamentum*, XVI (1974), 179–206.

Supper (*idion deipnon* vs. *kuriakon deipnon*). The error, as Paul sees it, is that they continue to regard it as their own. Therefore he repeats the words of institution (11:23ff.) to confirm that it should be regarded as the Lord's meal, to be partaken of by all.

Plutarch, the moral philosopher, shows us that the problem Theissen envisages was common enough in banquets. He describes a banquet in which guests brought their individual meals and complains that this resulted in many banquets and a consequent destruction of fellowship. "Where each guest has his own private portion, fellowship perishes."[46] This was the situation at Corinth, except that groups rather than individuals were involved; and the distinction was between the haves and the have-nots. The action of the haves, according to Paul, is tantamount to despising and humiliating those of lesser means. The situation was further aggravated when those who brought their own meals ate without waiting for the rest. Paul instructs them to eat at home if they are too hungry to wait (I Cor. 11:34).

Theissen thinks that the affluent members provided the food for the Lord's Supper but retained some food for themselves, which they began to eat before the Lord's Supper and continued to eat after the common meal started. Paul's warning that "any one who eats and drinks without discerning the body eats and drinks judgment upon himself" (I Cor. 11:29) is directed against this practice, which did not discriminate between the two types of food. The rich may have seen nothing incongruous in keeping more for themselves. It was not uncommon in the feasts of ancient associations for some members to be favored over others. But in the church in Corinth it was not done according to a regular order.

46. Plutarch *Table Talk* 644C.

Favoritism may further have been manifested in the types of foods distributed. The words of institution dealt only with bread and wine, and the well-to-do could have claimed that by providing bread and wine for others they were acting in accordance with the tradition that they had received from Paul. They would then have been free to keep for themselves any other quantities and delicacies they wished.[47] This practice, too, is discussed in ancient writings dealing with banquets. It was condemned, especially by the satirists, who criticized it from the perspective of the disadvantaged. The practice had the effect, and in some cases the intention, of demonstrating the different social levels of the participants. Although the Corinthian table fellowship was not a private meal, the participants were guests in Gaius' house; and it is conceivable that the practice, if not the specific rationale for it, may have created tension.

The well-to-do may have acted without any ignoble motives. They possibly thought that they were providing a service for the poor. The conflict was rooted in the fact that the social structure and the attendant behavior that it brought into the church collided with the Christian tradition's concept of the nature of community. Since Paul looks at the matter from below, the members from the upper strata do not appear in a good light in his letters to them. He does not, however, adopt a pragmatic approach in addressing himself to these problems. He does advise the well-to-do to eat at home, but their behavior in the fellowship meal, his chief concern, is viewed from a theo-

47. Theissen considers it possible (195f.) that, if the *idion deipnon* included meat, then I Corinthians 10:14–22 and 11:17ff. deal with the same problem—the eating of meat during the communal gatherings. The Lord's Supper cannot be combined with a meal that is either regarded as one's own or contains meat offered to idols. Both cases could be true, since one could not absolutely exclude the possibility that meat sold in Corinth had not been ritually slaughtered, and could therefore be regarded as "meat offered to idols." Theissen admits that the hypothesis needs the support of an exegesis of I Corinthians 8–10, which he does not provide.

logical perspective. The social divisions (I Cor. 11:19) are seen as part of the eschatological drama in which the just and the unjust are separated. The problems associated with the meal are not to be solved by the application of proper etiquette, but by working out their theological implications. The conduct of the well-to-do is not simply offensive to the others' sensitivities; it involves judgment (11:29–32). Through this type of instruction Paul aims at greater social integration within the community's celebration of the Lord's Supper.

III

Theissen's efforts to interpret the situation in Corinth are not always convincing. He is more successful in describing the social stratification of the Corinthian church than he is in relating it to the theological problems that beset it. But his sociological findings clearly indicate that social status most probably exacerbated those problems. The history of research does reveal a neglect of the sociological aspects of the Corinthians' problems, but it equally reveals that theological issues have been identified and explored successfully. Therefore Theissen's work provides a welcome new perspective from which to view those discussions, but it cannot be regarded as an alternative. It is not clear whether Theissen himself regards his approach as an alternative that can stand by itself without further attention to well-established viewpoints or to the texts, which he approaches solely with his sociological interest in mind.

Theissen's research is significant because of the change in focus that it represents. Judge, many of whose insights Theissen builds upon, remarked:

If the common assertion that the Christian groups were constituted from the lower orders of society is meant to imply that they did not draw upon the upper orders of the Roman ranking system, the observation is correct, and pointless. In the eastern Mediterranean it was self-evident that members of the Roman aristocracy would not belong to a cult association. . . . The only Roman aristocrats likely to be found in the east were the provincial governors themselves and a few members of their staffs; distinguished local politicians who had been elevated for their services in order that outstanding talent for leadership should have a vested interest in the Roman loyalty; and millionaires on business from the capital, together with the local magnates who attracted official attention by public benefactions.

Christians would only occasionally meet such people.[48]

Judge recently complained that "the Roman ranking system, headed by the senatorial and equestrian orders, has been extensively studied, and dominates our picture of the provinces, faute de mieux." He calls for the identification of the status of persons other than slaves to whom the New Testament writers address themselves. "Until we do so, the largely irrelevant picture we have of the metropolitan aristocracy will continue to lead to facile assumptions about the low level of Paul and his society."[49] This identification has now partially been supplied by Theissen, who is more concerned with the social level of influential converts to Christianity than with their ranking or legal status in the Roman system. Of significant value is his treatment of the customs and experiences of those levels of society that he believes acted upon the Christian fellowship.[50]

---

48. Judge, *Social Pattern of Christian Groups*, 52. Gülzow, "Soziale Gegebenheiten," 220f., represents the same view.

49. Judge, "St. Paul and Classical Society," 28. Gager, *Kingdom and Community*, 96ff., *passim*, has not succeeded in avoiding the trap. He follows J. Gagé, *Les classes sociales dans l'empire romain* (Paris, 1964), who focuses on the city of Rome "with the assumption that conditions there prevailed more or less uniformly throughout the empire." (p. 108 n. 3).

50. Theissen stresses the merchant class and neglects the slaves and freedmen who were members of the church. See Henneke Gülzow, *Christentum und Sklaverei in den ersten drei Jahrhunderten* (Bonn, 1969), esp. 41–46, 177ff., and S. Scott Bartchy, *Mallon chresai: First Century Slavery and the Interpretation of I Corinthians 7:21*, Society of Biblical Literature Dissertation Series, XI (Missoula, Mont., 1973).

The interest has shifted from the relationship between Christianity and Roman society, with each one being viewed as a homogeneous entity. The new focus on the social differentiation within the church marks a considerable advance.

A type of depiction of Roman society that would enrich our understanding of social relations, not only within the church, but between its members and different groups within Roman society, is provided by Ramsay MacMullen.[51] He points to the importance of wealth for social standing in Roman society. The property requirements for membership in the senatorial and equestrain orders were of such magnitude that those orders constituted far less than one-fifth of 1 percent of the total population of the Empire. While there was no middle class as we understand it, statistically there was one. "Between the top and bottom, taking into a single glance the entire empire, a range of intermediate wealth made up the aristocracy of small cities. In a given city, however, the aristocracy nevertheless stood upon the summit of a very steep social pyramid. The feel of society, the living sense of its proportions, thus did not harmonize with statistics."[52] At the bottom were the totally indigent, mostly free, but including slaves. Between the municipal aristocracy and the impoverished was a heterogeneous group that cannot be called a middle class. Although small tradesmen rarely acquired great fortunes, "people who started with some minor skill or minor sum of money could indeed rise to relative affluence."[53] The key to Roman society, according to MacMullen, is "verticality." The sense of high and low pressed heavily on people, and he vividly describes the tensions that existed between the different classes.

Representatives of the emerging consensus on the social sta-

51. MacMullen, *Roman Social Relations*, 88–120.
52. *Ibid.*, 89f. *Cf.*, Gülzow, "Soziale Gegebenheiten," 189.
53. MacMullen, *Roman Social Relations*, 99.

tus of early Christians view the church as comprising a cross section of most of Roman society. In that respect they consider the church to have been different from other ancient cults and associations, which they believe were more homogeneous in their membership and, therefore, unable to form satisfactory analogies to early Christian groups.[54] Their tendency is not to examine other groups as institutions, but to concentrate on the relationships between various members of society. This approach differs markedly from the efforts made in the nineteenth century to establish lines of development between the associations and the early church.[55]

Georg Heinrici presented the view that the church structured itself in the form of Greek associations.[56] The theory was further worked out by Edwin Hatch in his Bampton Lectures in 1880.[57] Although Heinrici and Hatch met with vigorous opposition,[58] their work is valuable, and we should become familiar with the associations and clubs that they considered

54. See, for example, Judge, *Social Pattern of Christian Groups*, 60; Theissen, "Soziale Schichtung," 268, and his "Soziale Integration," 180f. See Gager, *Kingdom and Community*, 99, in reference to a Dionysiac cult in which senators actively participated along with their clients, freedmen, and slaves: "Such cultic associations, especially those of Eastern origin, seem to have been the only areas in which social rank gave way to fellowship among different social groups. Even here, however, membership in the congregation included only the senators' immediate clients and households." The qualification is important. For a more detailed discussion, see Gülzow, "Soziale Gegebenheiten," 189ff., 219ff.

55. See p. 8 n. 16 herein.

56. The most important of a series of articles by Georg Heinrici on this subject are: "Die Christengemeinden Korinths und die religiösen Genossenschaften der Griechen," *Zeitschrift für wissenschaftliche Theologie*, XIX (1876), 465–526; "Zur Geschichte der Anfänge paulinischer Gemeinden," *ibid.*, XX (1877), 89–130; "Zum genossenschaftlichen Charakter der paulinischen Christengemeinden," *Theologische Studien und Kritiken*, LIV (1881), 505–24.

57. Edwin Hatch, *The Organization of the Early Christian Church* (London, 1918).

58. For a rejection of Heinrici's views, see Johannes Weiss, *Der erste Korintherbrief* (Göttingen, Germany, 1910), xx–xxix. For the opposition to Hatch, on the basis of theological rather than historical grounds, see N. F. Josaitis, *Edwin Hatch and Early Church Order* (Gembloux, Belgium, 1971).

so important and about which we now have more information.[59] It is significant that the influence of these associations on Jewish tradition can be detected[60] and that later in the history of the church both pagans[61] and Christians themselves[62] described Christinity as a *thiasos*, or confraternity, a term frequently used to denote the associations.

Since one segment of the Corinthian church consisted of craftsmen and tradesmen, one particular kind of association, a guild of tradesmen, may reward close investigation. These *collegia*, composed of men practicing the same trade, did not exist to improve their economic condition. Although the cultic aspect was not absent from their gatherings, the guilds' real purpose was to provide a social life for their members. "What is interesting about crafts associations for our purposes is the focusing of their energies on the pursuit of honor rather than of economic advantage. . . . Associations resembled the whole social context they found themselves in and imitated it as best they could." Within their organization they copied the ways of bestowing honor and also the terminology of larger political bodies. "At least the larger craft associations constituted in every detail miniature cities."[63] In them, unlike the cult asso-

59. *Cf.*, Weiss, *Der erste Korintherbrief*, xxii, and for recent treatments, the works of Ramsay MacMullen, *Enemies of the Roman Order and his Roman Social Relations*, and Alison Burford, *Craftsmen in Greek and Roman Society* (London, 1972).

60. See, for example, Hans Bardtke, "Der gegenwärtige Stand der Erforschung der in Palästina neu gefundenen hebräischen Handschriften, 44: Die Rechtsstellung der Qumran-Gemeinde," *Theologische Literaturzeitung*, LXXXVI (1961), 93–104; B. W. Dombrowski, *"yahad* in I QS and *to koinon*: An Instance of Early Greek and Jewish Synthesis," *Harvard Theological Review*, LIX (1966), 293–307; Martin Hengel, *Judaism and Hellenism*, trans. John Bowden (2 vols.; Philadelphia, 1974), I, 243ff.

61. For example, Lucian *Peregrinus* 11, and Celsus, according to Origen *Against Celsus* III, 23.

62. Tertullian *Apology* 39. On this passage, see R. L. Wilken, "Collegia, Philosophical Schools and Theology," in Stephen Benko and John J. O'Rourke (eds.), *The Catacombs and the Colosseum: The Roman Empire as the Setting of Primitive Christianity* (Valley Forge, Pa., 1971), 268–91.

63. MacMullen, *Roman Social Relations*, 77, 76.

ciations, were men of different social status who were conscious of the possibility of advancement. [64] Therefore, social stratification, which is so important to Theissen, is found in those associations to which the dominant Corinthian Christians had most likely belonged before their conversion.

Heinrici and Hatch pressed the evidence too far in their attempts to prove that the organization of the early church was in good measure derived from the associations. Given the scanty information about the structure of the early church, their enthusiasm was understandably regarded as excessive. Although the possibility of demonstrating a genealogical relationship between the organizations of the associations and the church is unlikely, the value of the material dealing with the associations is not vitiated. If we are interested in social relations rather than organizational structure, and in analogies rather than in genealogical relationships, the material may help to clarify some aspects of both the informal relationships within the church as well as the church's relationship to the larger society.

We have noted that in the second century, pagans and Christians did not consider it incongruous to speak explicitly of the church as a *thiasos*. It is possible that Luke, while not explicitly calling the church in Ephesus a guild, nevertheless shows it operating within the social milieu of guilds. Luke's account of the founding of the church in Ephesus has Paul continuing his teaching activity in the *schole* of Tyrannus after he withdraws from the synagogue (Acts 19:9). This *schole* is usually understood to have been a lecture hall, and it has been suggested that Paul is presented here as a wandering philosopher. [65] The evidence, however, suggests a different probabil-

64. F. Boemer, *Untersuchungen über die Religion der Sklaven in Griechenland und Rom* (4 vols.; Wiesbaden, Germany, 1963), IV, 240.

65. Hans Conzelmann, *Die Apostelgeschichte* (Tübingen, Germany, 1963), 198, and see *n*. 71 below.

ity. *Schola* was a common designation for a guild hall, which was frequently named for a guild's patron.[66] It is quite likely that Luke intends his readers to understand the hall of Tyrannus as a meeting place like that of the *collegia*.[67] His picture of Paul's activities in Ephesus supports the idea. Paul does not appear as a wandering philosopher during his sojourn in Ephesus, but as a workman who lives in contact with other craftsmen.[68] In Acts 18:3 Luke had described Aquila, Priscilla, and Paul as tentmakers working at their trade and going to Ephesus together (18:18ff.) In Acts 20:31–35 he writes that Paul claims to have engaged in manual labor during his stay in Ephesus, and extraordinary healings are said to have occurred through contact with cloths he used as aprons and sweat-rags during his work (19:11, 12).[69] Later, he comes in conflict with the

66. On guild halls and patrons, see J. P. Waltzing, *Étude historique sur les corporations professionelles chez les Romains* (4 vols.; Louvain, Belgium, 1895), I, 211ff., 415–46; Gaston Boissier, *La religion romaine d'Auguste aux Antonins* (5th ed.; Paris, 1900), 246ff.

67. Heinrich J. Holtzmann, *Die Pastoralbriefe* (Leipzig, Germany, 1880), 198, and see *n.* 71 below.

68. In his description of the Jerusalem church, Acts 4:32 (*cf.*, 2:44f.), Luke does use the terms "of one soul" (*mia psyche*) and "everything in common" (*panta koina*), which were commonly used to describe ideal philosophical communities. The material has been collected by H. von Schubert, *Der Kommunismus der Wiedertäufer in Münster und seine Quellen* (Heidelberg, 1911); *Theological Dictionary of the New Testament, s.v. "koinos"*; Eckhard Plümacher, *Lukas als hellenistischer Schriftsteller* (Göttingen, Germany, 1972), 16ff. Luke's description of Peter and John, the leaders of that community, as "uneducated, common men" (Acts 4:13), is in accord with the common popular-philosophical (*sc.* Cynic) dictum that the life of simple men is best. *Cf.*, Lucian *Menippus* 21; Rudolf Helm, *Lucian und Menipp* (Leipzig-Berlin, 1906), 37f. Luke's use of that theme may already reflect the intent it assumed in later Christian apologetic. *Cf.*, Athenagoras *Plea* 11 (p. 128, l. 18ff) in the Geffcken edition. On *Plea* 11, see Abraham J. Malherbe, "Athenagoras on Christian Ethics," *Journal of Ecclesiastical History*, XX (1969), 1ff. On Acts 4, see further Dielfried Gewalt, "Neutestamentliche Exegese und Soziologie," *Evangelische Theologie*, XXXI (1971), esp. 90ff.

69. On this interpretation of the verse, see Franz Overbeck's comment in W. M. L. de Wette, *Kurze Erklärung der Apostelgeschichte* (4th ed.; Leipzig, Germany, 1870), 315; F. F. Bruce, *Commentary on the Book of Acts* (Grand Rapids, Mich., 1956), 389.

guild of silversmiths (19:23ff.). In the face of the many problems posed by Acts 19, it is difficult to fit all the details into one purpose that Luke might have had in giving this account; but it does seem clear that the economic motive for the opposition to Christians is basic. [70] This reading of the evidence places Paul squarely in the kind of environment Theissen has suggested for the church in Corinth. It also shows that, in view of Luke's representation, the guilds deserve further attention. It has often been suggested that the house church is analogous to household *collegia*. [71] If the view here presented is correct, house churches should be examined in light of the relationship between *collegia* and household communities.

70. On the economic ties of particular trades as contributing to the formation of communities in certain sections of cities, see MacMullen, *Roman Social Relations*, 69f. On quarrels between guilds, and on Acts 19:23ff., see MacMullen, *Enemies of the Roman Order*, 342 n. 16.

71. It has often been suggested that the house church is analogous to the associations referred to in *Corpus Inscriptionum Latinarum* 9148, *collegium quod est in domo Sergiae Paullinae*. Cf., Ernest Renan, *Paulus* (Leipzig, Germany, 1869), 257; W. Liebenam, *Zur Geschichte und Organisation des römischen Vereinswesens* (Leipzig, Germany, 1890), 272 n. 4.

4

Hospitality
and Inhospitality
in the Church*

A^N AWARENESS of the social dimension of early Christianity may help us in our attempts at historical reconstruction by providing new information and exercising discipline over our efforts. The latter is especially important in view of the tendency to construct vast developmental systems on the basis of very slender evidence, or to fit texts into elaborate reconstructions. Third John has been subjected to such treatment, and in this chapter I shall attempt to cast light on this controverted document by examining it in the same way I did I Thessalonians (pp. 20–28); that is, I shall pay close attention to the social practices reflected in the letter and to the literary genre and function of the document.

The major controversy revolves around Diotrephes. Despite the fact that our knowledge of him is confined to what is said of him in III John 9f., he has been regarded as of great importance because he provides us with a glimpse into the devel-

*This chapter appeared in substantially the same form under the title "The Inhospitality of Diotrephes," in *God's Christ and His People: Studies in Honour of Nils Alstrup Dahl,* ed. Jacob Jervell and Wayne A. Meeks (Oslo: Universitetsforlaget, 1977), 222–32. I am grateful for permission to reprint it here.

opment of early Christianity at the end of the first century. The attempts to place him in his proper context have resulted in quite diverse interpretations of what is said about him.[1]

A traditional interpretation, represented by Theodor Zahn, held that Diotrephes was an autocratic bishop who had the power of excommunication (v. 10, "he puts them out of the church").[2] What Diotrephes is accused of, according to this interpretation, is not that he does not have the authority to excommunicate, but that he employs it in an imperious and ruinous manner.

Adolf Harnack saw the chief importance of III John in the information it affords us with regard to the development of church organization in Asia Minor.[3] On the one hand is the Elder who exercises great influence over the churches in the region, using his traveling emissaries as a means of control over them. On the other is Diotrephes who, with the majority of his church, rejects the authority of the Elder by refusing to receive his emissaries. This Harnack regards as evidence of the consolidation of individual churches and the rejection of the old provincial mission organization. Diotrephes, according to this interpretation, is the first monarchical bishop whose name we know.

More recently the tendency has been to find theological motives for Diotrephes' actions. Walter Bauer placed Diotrephes in the struggle between "orthodoxy" and "heresy," making him a representative of the latter.[4] On this understanding, Dio-

1. See Ernst Haenchen, "Neuere Literatur zu den Johannesbriefen," *Theologische Rundschau*, N. F., XXVI(1960), 268–91.
2. Theodor Zahn, *Introduction to the New Testament* (repr. 1953), III, 375ff.
3. Adolf Harnack, "Uber den dritten Johannesbrief," vol. XV, 3 of *Texte und Untersuchungen* (Berlin, 1897).
4. Walter Bauer, *Orthodoxy and Heresy in Earliest Christianity*, ed. Robert A. Kraft and Gerhard Krodel, trans. Philadelphia Seminar on Christian Origins (Philadelphia, 1971), 93f.

trephes takes the same action against the emissaries of the Elder that the latter in II John 10f. had prescribed against docetists. Ernst Käsemann is also convinced that the issue between the Elder and Diotrephes was not merely personal or a matter of church organization, but in fact theological.[5] However, he stands Bauer's theory on its head: Diotrephes was theologically traditional, the Elder innovative. This is proven for him by the fact that the Elder does not accuse Diotrephes of heresy, which one would have expected him to do had Diotrephes been heretical. He further suggests that Diotrephes had excommunicated the Elder, and that his authority was therefore recognized by Diotrephes' church and by the Elder, who had formerly been a member of it.

In the absence of unambiguous information that can serve as a control, the temptation is always to fit Diotrephes into a preconceived scheme, and none of these interpretations successfully resists it. Given the paucity of information about Diotrephes, the most that can be claimed for any of these theories by their proponents is that they may be probable. Acknowledging that we are limited to probabilities, I suggest that we attempt to understand Diotrephes in light of the main subject of III John, which is the extension of hospitality to fellow Christians. That is the point at issue, and by examining what is said of Diotrephes from the perspective of the practice in the New Testament we may hope to attain some clarity on his actions.

I

The practice of private hospitality was widely recognized as a virtue in antiquity, but may have declined as such in the

5. Ernst Käsemann, "Ketzer und Zeuge. Zum johanneischen Verfassers-problem," *Zeitschrift für Theologie und Kirche*, XLVIII(1951), 292–311 (=*Exegetische Versuche und Besinnungen*, 1 [Göttingen, 1965], 168–87) and *Exegetische Versuche und Besinnungen*, 2 (1965[2]), 133 n. 1.

pagan world of the first century A.D.[6] The mobility which characterized the period brought with it a system of inns which sought to meet the needs and desires of travelers. The inns, however, did not enjoy a good reputation among the upper classes, being considered centers of all sorts of nefarious activities and offering poor service.[7] Whenever possible, therefore, discriminating travelers availed themselves of the hospitality of business associates and other acquaintances.[8]

The early church reflects the mobility of Roman society as well as the practice of private hospitality. The Book of Acts presents Paul as establishing churches on the main trade routes of the Empire and having among his first associates and converts people who were, like himself, transients. Paul's own letters further impress one with the mobility of his co-workers.[9] It is understandable that, in view of conditions in the inns,

6. See Gustav Stählin, *Theological Dictionary of the New Testament*, V, 1–36, *s.v. "xenos"*; Helga Rusche, *Gastfreundschaft in der Verkündigung des neuen Testaments und ihr Verhältnis zur Mission* (Münster, Germany, 1957); and especially J. B. Mathews, "Hospitality and the New Testament Church: An Historical and Exegetical Study" (Th.D. Dissertation, Princeton Theological Seminary, 1965). Mathews's view (180ff.) of the decline should be modified in light of such experiences as Dio Chrysostom (*Oration 7*) enjoyed among the poor peasants on Euboea. See also Donald W. Riddle, "Early Christian Hospitality: A Factor in the Gospel Transmission," *Journal of Biblical Literature*, LVII(1938), 141–54.

7. The most useful study of travel conditions for our purpose is still that of W. M. Ramsay, "Roads and Travel (in the New Testament)," *Hastings Dictionary of the Bible*, V(1904), 375–402. For conditions in the inns, see T. Kleberg, *Hôtels, restaurants et cabarets dans l'antiquité romaine* (Uppsala, Sweden, 1957); and T. Crane, *"Caveat Viator*: Roman Country Inns," *Classical Bulletin*, XLVI(1969), 6ff.

8. See Horace, *Satire* I, v, for a colorful account of a journey from Rome to Brundisium.

9. For the trade routes, see Ramsay, "Roads and Travel," *Hastings Dictionary*. Of Paul's associates, Aquila and Prisca are at various times placed in Pontus, Rome, Corinth, and Ephesus (Acts 18:1–3, 18f.). Lydia is associated with Thyatira and Philippi (Acts 16:14). For his co-workers, see E. Earle Ellis, "Paul and His Co-Workers," *New Testament Studies*, XVII(1971), 437–52. Harry Y. Gamble, *The Textual History of the Letter to the Romans* (Grand Rapids, Mich., 1977), has convincingly shown that Romans 16 was part of Paul's original letter to Rome. The number of people Paul greets in that chapter, whom he had known in the eastern Medi-

Christian travelers would prefer to avail themselves of the hospitality of their brethren. The Book of Acts shows a social interest in the practice; it is presupposed in Paul's letters as he plans his own as well as his co-workers' travels, and it appears frequently in paraenesis.[10] A virtually technical vocabulary developed to describe the hospitable reception (compounds of *lambano* and *dechomai*) and sending on (*propempo*) of those individuals who were spreading the faith.[11]

In addition to the material support of travelers, Christian hospitality was further manifested in the phenomenon of the house church. In its earliest period the churches had no buildings especially designed for their religious services and seem to have met primarily in hospitable homes.[12] The Book of Acts

terranean but who find themselves in Rome at the time of writing, illustrates most impressively the mobility of the church.

10. For hospitality in Acts, see *e.g.* Acts 21:4, 7, 16f., and Henry J. Cadbury, "Lexical Notes on Luke-Acts," *Journal of Biblical Literature,* XLV(1926), 305–22; and *The Making of Luke-Acts* (London, repr. 1958), 251ff. See Rom. 15:28f.; 16:1f.; I Cor. 16:10f.; Phil. 2:29; Philemon 22 for hospitality in travel plans, and Rom. 12:13; Heb. 13:2; I Pet. 4:9 for it in paraenesis.

11. See Mathews, *Hospitality and the New Testament Church,* 166–74. *Lambano* and its cognates are used in this sense especially in the Johannine literature: *lambano,* II John 10; *hupolambano,* III John 8, *cf.* Josephus, *Against Apion* 1.247; *proslambano,* Acts 28:2; Philemon 17. *Dechomai* and its cognates are also used in this sense: *dechomai,* Mark 6:11 and parallels; Col. 4:10, *cf. Didache* 11:1f.; *apodechomai,* Acts 18:27; 21:17; *prosdechomai,* Rom. 16:2; Phil. 2:29; *anadechomai,* Acts 28:7; *hupodechomai,* Acts 17:7, *cf.* Ignatius, *Letter to the Smyrnaeans* 10:1; Hermas, *Similitudines* VIII, 10, 3; IX,27,2; *epidechomai,* III John 10. *Propempo* is used in the New Testament only for sending a departing traveler on his way. It could mean accompanying him for a short distance (Acts 20:38; 21:5) or simply sending him on a mission (Acts 15:3), but more generally it means to equip him with all things necessary for the journey (Tit. 3:13; *cf.* Rom. 15:24; I Cor. 16:6, 11; II Cor. 1:16; III John 6; Polycarp, *Philippians* 1:1), and is thus almost synonymous with *ephodiazo* (*cf.* Josephus, *Jewish War* 2.103; *Jewish Antiquities* 20.50). For the practice, also see Acts 28:10. *Cf.* Zahn, *Introduction to the New Testament,* 54 *n.* 4; Mathews, *Hospitality and the New Testament Church,* 230f.

12. See Floyd V. Filson, "The Significance of Early House Churches," *Journal of Biblical Literature,* LVIII(1939), 105–12; Oscar Cullmann, *Early Christian Worship* (London, 1953), 9f.; E. A. Judge, *The Social*

represents Paul as converting entire households and using them as bases for his missionary activity, and Paul's letters reveal that his churches continued to meet in the homes of some of their members.[13] The arrangement had its positive side, the implications of which have not yet sufficiently been investigated. But it was also beset with problems, which are of more immediate interest to us.[14]

Among the problems is the role of the Christian patron in whose house the church would meet. To have had house churches implies that there were Christians of sufficient means to provide large enough quarters for the church's meetings. We know from Paul's letters of at least two such hosts who extended hospitality both to a local group of Christians as well as to traveling Christians, in this case, Paul himself (Rom. 16:23; Philemon 2, 22). From the events in Thessalonica (Acts 17: 5–9) we know that such patrons assumed legal responsibility for the groups meeting in their houses.[15] Exactly what status in the congregations which met in their houses this service conferred on them is not totally clear. An answer to that ques-

---

Pattern of Christian Groups in the First Century (London, 1960), esp. Chapter V; Richard Krautheimer, *Early Christian and Byzantine Architecture* (Baltimore, 1965), 1ff.; Leonhard Goppelt, *Apostolic and Post-Apostolic Times* (New York, 1970), 88, 204f. Michael Green, *Evangelism in the Early Church* (London, 1970), 81, 207–23, 326, provides a useful collection of evidence although his interpretation is not always satisfactory.

13. *Cf.* Acts 18:1–8; 17:6f.; 16:15, 31ff.; I Cor. 1:14–16; 16:19; Rom. 16:3ff.; Col. 4:15; Philemon 2, etc.

14. For the implications of the house church, see Filson, "Significance of Early Christian Houses." For how an understanding of the social structure of a house church can illuminate our understanding of I Corinthians, see Gerd Theissen, *The Social Setting of Pauline Christianity* (Philadelphia, 1982), 69–174. One of the major problems was that if whole households could be converted, they could also be led astray, a concern of the Pastoral Epistles (*cf.* Tit. 1:11; II Tim. 3:6).

15. *Labontes to hikanon* is the equivalent of *satis accipere*, in Roman criminal and civil law the posting of a bond which could be forfeited if the offense were repeated. *Cf.* Kirsopp Lake and Henry J. Cadbury, *The Beginnings of Christianity* (London, 1933), IV, 206; A. N. Sherwin-White, *Roman Society and Roman Law in the New Testament* (Oxford, 1963), 95f.

tion involves one's understanding of the meaning of *proistemi* in its various contexts in the New Testament, a matter that cannot be gone into in detail here. It would appear certain that in the Pauline letters the term does not denote an office. In Romans 12:8 and I Thessalonians 5:12 it means to give aid. Phoebe is described in Romans 16:2 as *prostatis*, that is, a legal representative of the church, very much like Jason was in Thessalonica.[16] The description most likely implies that she hosted a church in her house as he did. Given Paul's view of the lack of authority of women in the church (I Cor. 14:33–37), his description of Phoebe as "patroness (*prostatis*) of many and myself as well" makes it clear that he does not view a patron(ess) of the church as having authority by virtue of his or her care for the church.

The Pastoral Epistles may, on the surface, seem to provide more information.[17] They are concerned with heresy, especially as it was making inroads into Christian households (II Tim. 3:16; Tit. 1:11). It is striking how frequently *oikos* ("house") and its cognates appear in the letters.[18] The church order which the letters advance is designed to strengthen the church in its battle with heresy.[19] The church is described as the "household of God" (I Tim. 3:15; *cf.* II Tim. 2:20) in which the bishop serves "as God's household manager" (Tit. 1:7). The qualifications for the various functionaries in the church—whether the bishops, deacons, or widows—always involve their behavior in, or the circumstances of, their own

16. See W. Sanday and A. C. Headlam, *The Epistle to the Romans* (Edinburgh, 1908), 417f., and Bo Reicke, *Diakonie, Festfreude und Zelos* (Uppsala, Sweden, 1951), 244 *n.* 8, on Phoebe as *prostatis* of the church in Cenchreae.

17. See Bo Reicke, *Theological Dictionary of the New Testament*, VI, 700–703, *s.v.* "*proistemi.*"

18. I Tim. 3:4, 5, 12, 15; 5:4, 8, 13, 14; II Tim. 2:20; Tit. 1:7, 11.

19. Note I Tim. 3:14ff. and Tit. 1:10ff., following the lists of qualifications.

households (I Tim. 3:4f., 12; 5:4). Deacons are required to be *teknon kalos proistamenoi kai ton idion oikon* (I Tim. 3: 12), where the meaning must be to take care of their own households.[20] A similar requirement is made of the bishops, and its purpose is clearly stated: "for if a man does not know how to take care of (*prostenai*) his own household, how could he care (*epimelesetai*) for God's church?" (I Tim. 3:4f.). The meaning of *prostenai* may here shade into that of "to manage," but, as *epimelesetai* would indicate, the element of care is still present.[21]

It is difficult to obtain a clear picture of the social circumstances of the churches addressed in the Pastoral Epistles. It is tempting, in view of the requirement that the bishop be hospitable (I Tim. 3:2; Tit. 1:8; *cf.* Hermas, *Sim* IX, 27, 2), of the description of the church as the household of God, and of the stress on the household, to assume that bishops had churches in their homes and there exercised rule over them. But there is nothing in the Pastorals to compel such an idea. If we are to assume that such a host would be financially well-off and generous, I Timothy 5:17f. might be read as contrary evidence, for there the elder is the recipient of material reward, not the provider for the church.[22] Be that as it may, the Pastorals do not provide evidence that the bishops derived authority from providing hospitality to the church.[23] What authority they may have had they derived elsewhere. Furthermore, the

20. Reicke, *Theological Dictionary*, s.v. *"proistemi,"* 702: Although the *patria potestas* is assumed, attention is rather drawn to the care of the deacon's family.

21. The move from household to broader responsibilities is a hellenistic paraenetic commonplace. *Cf.* H. Almqvist, *Plutarch und das Neue Testament* (Uppsala, Sweden, 1946), 125, but that should not by itself be taken to mean that it has no relevance to the situation at hand.

22. I assume, on the basis of Tit. 1:5ff., that the *episkopoi* and *presbuteroi* are the same individuals.

23. From Tit. 3:12–14 it appears that it is the responsibility of all Christians to speed travelers on their way (*propempo*), not of the bishops only.

actions to be taken against the heretics, unlike that commended in II John 10, are not explicitly described in terms of the refusal of hospitality to them either by the church or the bishop. Rather, the author's overriding concern is that they be avoided and, when they are confronted, the contact with them be limited to one or two encounters.[24] One may expect that hospitality would have been refused them as in II John 10, but that raises the question where two admonitions of them could be expected to take place (Tit. 3:10). We must conclude, then, that the evidence of the Pastoral Epistles is unclear so far as the house church and its patron is concerned.

The information on the number of house churches within one locality and their relationship to each other is scanty.[25] But we do have some information that permits us a glimpse, if no more, of the situation in the different parts of the Roman Empire. It is generally thought that Paul in Romans 16 is aware of at least three house churches in the community to which he writes (vv. 5, 14, 15),[26] and Colossians 4:15 may indicate that there was more than one church in Laodicea.[27] Paul's admonition that I Thessalonians be read "to all the brethren" (5:27; cf. Col. 4:16) may indicate a plurality of groups in Thessalonica. In that case, and on the acceptance of the early dating of I Thessalonians, we would have evidence that a number of separate groups had developed soon after the church's establishment. We do not know much about the rela-

24. Cf. I Tim. 4:7; 6:11; II Tim. 2:14, 16, 23; 3:6; Tit. 1:11, 13; 3:9f.
25. Cf. Adolf Harnack, *The Mission and Expansion of Christianity in the First Three Centuries* (New York, 1908), I, 442ff.; II, 84ff. He does not, however, examine the New Testament material in detail.
26. E.g., Sanday and Headlam, *Epistle to the Romans*, 421; Judge, *Social Pattern*, 36.
27. Thus Ernst Lohmeyer, *Die Briefe an die Kolosser und an Philemon* (Göttingen, Germany, 1956), 169f. W. G. Kümmel, *Introduction to the New Testament* (14th rev. ed.; Nashville, 1965), 238, referring to Col. 4:15, 17 and Philemon 2, claims that two house churches in Colossae are mentioned. I take this to mean that he thinks Nympha also lived in Colossae. The majority opinion places her in Laodicea.

tionship between such groups except that the letters addressed to them are aware of their separate existence yet consider them united in such a way that one letter to each locality suffices for all the groups.[28] One may further suppose that by the time Acts and the Pastorals were written, there would have been more than one house church in any particular locality, yet these documents describe presbyters and bishops with respect to cities, not individual groups.[29] It would appear, then, that although there may have been a number of Christian groups in a particular locality they were not isolated from each other, but thought of themselves as together constituting the church in that location.[30]

The Christian practice of hospitality was open to abuses, as not only they but also pagans were aware.[31] As one way to regulate the practice to some degree, at least, letters of recom-

28. This is clearly the case with Romans 16. The letter *ek Laodikeias* ("from Laodicea"; Col. 4:16) was probably a letter addressed to Laodicea, *ek* indicating that the letter was to be brought from Laodicea to Colossae. *Cf.* Eduard Lohse, *Colossians and Philemon.* Hermeneia—A Critical and Historical Commentary on the Bible (Philadelphia, 1971), 174 *n.* 47. Were Colossians genuine, we would have two letters written to the same locality, but even then the personal circumstances attending the writing of Philemon, viz., the return of Onesimus to his master, would explain the necessity of two letters. Adolf Harnack, "Das Problem des zweiten Thessalonicherbriefs," *Sitzungsberichte Akademie Berlin,* Phil. hist. Kl., 1910, 560–78, correctly, I think, surmised the existence of at least two different groups in Thessalonica, but his theory that I and II Thessalonians were written to those different groups has rightly been rejected, most recently by Ernest Best, *A Commentary on the First and Second Epistles to the Thessalonians* (London, 1972), 38ff.

29. Acts 20:17. *Kat' ekklesian,* "church by church," in 14:23, in light of the mention of the cities evangelized in vv. 21f., should be taken in the same way. *Cf.* also Tit. 1:5.

30. See N. Afanasieff, "L'assemblée eucharistique unique dans l'église ancienne," *Kleronomia,* VI(1974), 1–36, for the argument that there was only one eucharistic gathering despite the existence of a number of groups. His argument that *kat' oikon ekklesia* should not be translated "house church," but "église locale qui se réunit dans une maison," is not convincing.

31. Second John 10 and *Didache* 11f. show the dangers inherent in the practice. For a pagan view of how Christian hospitality could be abused, see Lucian, *Peregrinus,* 11ff.

mendation were written to introduce traveling missionaries to the churches along their way. The custom of writing such letters was widespread in the first century. A recent study of familiar letters of recommendation by Chan-Hie Kim has enabled us to come to a better understanding of their form and content.[32] Many passages in the New Testament refer to the practice of writing such letters, and on the basis of form and content Kim identifies certain portions of Paul's letters as being related to the commendation and introduction.[33] The only non-Pauline passages of commendation that he finds in the New Testament are III John 12 and Hebrews 13:17. His analysis of the epistolary type shows that Paul's commendations follow, *mutatis mutandis*, the pattern of other letters of the same type. We are concerned with the elements in the letters rather than with the form of the letters. There are some features of the letter of recommendation that are of interest to us.

The person recommended is frequently identified as being an intimate of the writer. "By identifying himself with the recommended [person], the writer intends the recommendation to be taken as if he himself were being recommended. The sender hopes that the recipient will treat the person whom he has recommended just like himself."[34] Statements such as that in PapOslo 55, "receiving (*hupodexamenos*) him as though he were me," are common. The recipient is, then, on

32. Chan-Hie Kim, *The Familiar Letter of Recommendation* (Missoula, Mont., 1972), 119ff.
33. Acts 9:2; 18:27; 22:5; I Cor. 16:3 refer to the practice. See also Rom. 16:1–2 (possibly 3–16); I Cor. 16:15–16, 17–18; Phil. 2:29–30; 4:2–3; I Thess. 5:12–13a; Philemon (particularly 8–17).
34. Chan-Hie Kim, *Familiar Letter*, 50ff. He draws attention to Pap-Oxyrhychus 32, *peto domine et eum ante oculos habeas tamquam me;* Cicero, *To His Friends* XIII, 62, *cura ut habeas quo meo,* and to Pap-Oxyrhychus 1663 and PapRylands 691. See also Philemon 17, *proslabou auton hos eme.*

occasion asked to do what is requested for the sake of the writer.[35] The requests are made for general assistance, expressed in forms of *sunergeo* ("work with") and *lambano* ("receive"),[36] but quite frequently the request is more specific, for example, to extend hospitality to the recommended person who is the bearer of the letter. Such requests are expressed by compounds of *dechomai* ("receive") and other explicit statements on hospitality.[37] One reason given for fulfilling the request is that the recommended person may testify (*martureo*) to the writer of the good reception with which he had met.[38]

II

It is against this background, I suggest, that III John should be viewed. It is a real letter, addressed to a situation the author plans to correct.[39] It follows one that he had earlier written to the same church (v. 9). That letter appears to have been a letter of recommendation written on behalf of traveling brethren (vv. 5–8, 10).[40] Such a letter would have contained

35. See C. W. Keyes, "The Greek Letter of Introduction," *American Journal of Philology,* LVI(1935), 41: PapOxyrhychus 787, *eis ten emen katalogen poieseis auto*; pseudo-Plato, *Epistle* 15 (p. 532 Hercher), *hemon heneka*; Cicero, *To His Friends* XIII,78, *mea causa; ibid.,* XIII,31, *honoris mei causa.* See Chan-Hie Kim, *Familiar Letter,* 80f. for more references, and *cf.* Rom. 16:2, *prostatis . . . emou autou,* and Phil. 2:30.

36. *Sunergeo:* PapSocItal 376, 969. Note how frequently *sunergos* appears in the context of Pauline recommendations: Rom. 16:3, 9; Phil. 4:4; I Cor. 16:16; Philemon 24. *Antilambano:* PapSocItal 520; PapColumbia-Zenon 112.

37. *Hupodechomai:* PapOslo 55; PapPrinceton 105; *prosdechomai:* Pap-MilanVogliano 76; PapOslo 51, and Rom. 16:2; Phil. 2:29.

38. PapOslo 55; PapFlorence 173; PapOxyrhychus 1064; 1424.

39. C. H. Dodd, *The Johannine Epistles* (London, 1946), lxiii; Haenchen, "Neuere Literatur," 281f. *Cf.* the excellent article by Robert W. Funk, "The Form and Structure of II and III John," *Journal of Biblical Literature,* LXXXVI(1967), 424–30.

40. Thus Dodd, *Johannine Epistles,* 161f.; J. Chaine, *Les épitres catholiques* (Paris, 1939); Haenchen, "Neuere Literatur," 283; Rudolf Schnackenburg, *Die Johannesbriefe* (Freiburg, Germany, 1970), 326; Rudolf Bult-

the main elements common to letters of recommendation as enumerated above. The travelers had met with a mixed response from the people to whom the letter had been addressed. Gaius had received them and was then commended by the Elder in a manner that calls to mind the main elements of his earlier letter (vv. 5–8): "they testified (*emarturesan*) to your love," "to send them on their journey" (*propempsai*) "to receive hospitably" (*hupolambanein*), "fellow workers" (*sunergoi*). Diotrephes, however, had rejected the letter and its bearers (vv. 9, 10). This raises the question of the relationship between Gaius and Diotrephes. The letter had been addressed to the church, and it is to be assumed that Gaius knew about the letter.[41] There is no indication that Gaius held an official position in the church, although he does seem to have been an influential man with a circle of "friends" (*philoi*).[42] We can thus identify two groups: Gaius and his friends, and Diotrephes and those over whom he exercised some control. The relationship between the two groups is not spelled out, but it is unlikely that Gaius and his friends were part of the group dominated by Diotrephes.[43] There is no hint of a confronta-

mann, *The Johannine Epistles* (Philadelphia, 1973), 100. This is not a reference to II John, as has been argued by Zahn, *Introduction to the New Testament*, III, 375ff. The circumstances envisaged in the two are quite different.

41. There is no reason to suppose that Diotrephes had suppressed the letter, as is frequently assumed. Schnackenburg, *Die Johannesbriefe*, 326, is probably correct: the Elder mentions the letter only to point up the arrogance of Diotrephes.

42. For the Johannine sense of *philos*, see Gustav Stählin, *Theological Dictionary of the New Testament*, IX, 166, s.v. "*phileo.*" Zahn, *Introduction to the New Testament*, III, 375, represents the generally held opinion that there is no hint that Gaius occupies an official position in the church. *Ergazomai* in the commendation of Gaius in v. 5, *ho ean ergase*, does not describe an official or semiofficial activity, but rather the voluntary charitable service for someone as it does in Matt. 26:10; Gal. 6:10; Col. 3:23. Cf. Schnackenburg, *Die Johannesbriefe*, 323 n. 5.

43. Contra Schnackenburg, *Die Johannesbriefe*, 323, 328; Bultmann, *Johannine Epistles*, 95, 103; M. de Jonge, *De Brieven van Johannes* (Nijkerk, Holland, 1968), 256.

tion between Gaius and Diotrephes or of tension between them. Gaius had some knowledge of Diotrephes' group, but he was not a member of it, and not one of those whom Diotrephes ejected from the church because they wished to receive the traveling brethren (v. 10).[44] It is more reasonable to assume that there were at least two Christian groups in the immediate area, one associated with Gaius, the other with Diotrephes.[45] This would be in keeping with earlier evidence that a number of separate groups would soon be formed in one locality, and would eliminate the difficulties involved in placing Gaius in Diotrephes' group.

If the Elder had followed what appears to have been earlier practice and had addressed his former letter to all the house congregations which together constituted the church in the immediate region, it would explain Gaius's knowledge of its content without his having been a member of Diotrephes' church. But why, then, does he now write to Gaius without including the other groups? He may be doing so to encourage Gaius, but more to the point is that III John is itself a letter of recommendation, probably on behalf of Demetrius (vv. 11, 12). The Elder is certain that Demetrius will be as well received by Gaius as the earlier travelers had been. Third John is, then, at once a commendation of Gaius for his earlier hospitality, and a recommendation of Demetrius.[46] It should further be noted that, although it is a personal letter, v. 15 would indicate that it has a wider reference than Gaius alone.[47]

Diotrephes' actions become clearer when his relationship

44. Thus Dodd, *Johannine Epistles*, 161; Hans Windisch, *Die katholischen Briefe* (Tübingen, Germany, 1951), 140.
45. *Cf.* Schnackenburg, *Die Johannesbriefe*, 301; Maurice Goguel, *The Primitive Church* (London, 1964), 139.
46. *Cf.* U. von Wilamowitz-Moellendorff, "Lesefrüchte," *Hermes*, XXXIII(1898), 529ff.; Zahn, *Introduction to the New Testament*, III, 374; Schnackenburg, *Die Johannesbriefe*, 330.
47. *Cf.* also Philemon, which is more than a purely personal letter. See Lohse, *Colossians and Philemon*, 187.

with the Elder on one hand, and with his congregation on the other, is observed. Despite the efforts to prove otherwise, there is nothing in III John to suggest that the issue between the Elder and himself was a doctrinal one. The frequency with which "truth" occurs (vv. 1, 3, 4, 8, 12) does reflect the Elder's concern with pure doctrine,[48] but it is not an issue between the Elder and Diotrephes. Rather, it is the Elder's means of strengthening his recommendation of Demetrius to Gaius, that they might become "fellow workers in the truth" (v. 8; cf. 12). What is at issue is Diotrephes' refusal to receive the letter of recommendation that had been written: "but Diotrephes, who likes to put himself first (*philoproteuon*) among them, does not welcome (*epidechetai*) us." The Elder seems to think that Diotrephes had seen in the letter a threat to his own preeminence in the church, and that he had therefore rejected the letter as well as its bearers.

There is no reason to understand *epidechomai* in v. 9 as meaning "to recognize someone's authority," and in v. 10 as "to receive someone as guest."[49] In letters of recommendation, such as the letter referred to in v. 9, the request on behalf of the persons recommended was that they be received for the sake of the writer. The reception of such letters and their bearers was proof of the good will of the recipients, as I Maccabees and Josephus illustrate. The author of I Maccabees, writing of the friendship between the Jews and the Romans and Spartans, gives an account of the correspondence that passed between the various parties and the treatment of their emissaries.

48. This is stressed by Zahn, *Introduction to the New Testament;* Käsemann, "Ketzer und Zeuge"; and J. L. Houlden, *The Johannine Epistles* (New York, 1973), 8ff.
49. Thus William F. Arndt and F. Wilbur Gingrich, *A Greek-English Lexicon of the New Testament* (Chicago, 1957), s.v. *"epidechomai."* J. E. Huther, *Kritisch exegetisches Handbuch über die drei Briefe des Apostel Johannes* (Göttingen, Germany, 1868), 294, and de Jonge, *De Brieven van Johannes,* 263, correctly insist on the same meaning for both verses.

Of the Roman treatment of Jewish emissaries it is said (12:4): "And they gave the letters to the people in every place, asking them to provide (*propemposin*) for the envoys safe conduct to the land of Judah." The author indicates that the Jews had reciprocated. In a letter from Jonathan the high priest to the Spartans he has Jonathan remind them of the way Onias the high priest on a previous occasion had received a messenger from Arius the Spartan king (12:8). "Onias welcomed (*epedexato*) the envoy with honor, and received (*elabe*) the letter, which contained a clear declaration of alliance and friendship." Josephus's version of the incident, identifying the messenger as Demoteles, reads, "we glady received (*edexametha*) the letter and showed ourselves kindly disposed toward both Demoteles and Arius" (*Antiquities* 13.167). The reception of the letter and its bearer proved the good will of the recipient toward the writer.

It is such an understanding of *epidechomai* that is present in vv. 9 and 10. Diotrephes had shown his ill will toward the Elder by refusing his letter and his emissaries.[50] In addition, he slandered the Elder and, adding insult to injury, imposed his will on the brethren who would act contrary to his wishes. We must be content with the fact that we do not know what Diotrephes' reasons were for his conduct. We are limited to the Elder's view of the matter, and he sees it as a purely personal issue.

Of Diotrephes' actions with respect to his church, the Elder says, "he refuses himself to welcome (*epidechetai*) the brethren, and also stops those who want to welcome them and puts

50. It is probably significant that III John, which is itself a letter of recommendation, does not request that hospitality be extended to the traveling brethren for the sake of the Elder. Instead, Diotrephes is threatened with (v. 10) and Gaius is promised (vv. 13ff.) a personal visit. It is noteworthy that even in recommending the brethren to Gaius, he offers theological rather than personal reasons for doing so.

them out of the church" (*ek tes ekklesias ekballei*) (v. 10). As we have seen, Diotrephes' action has been described as excommunication, an action which was in his power as monarchical bishop.[51] Nothing is said in the text, however, of any office that he may have occupied. That he was a monarchical bishop is often concluded from the description of him as "[someone] who likes to put himself first" (*philoproteuon*) (v. 9) and the statement, "he puts them out of the church" (*ek tes ekklesias ekballei*) (v. 10). But *philoproteuo* can mean either to be ambitious to become first (*protos*) or to love being first.[52] By itself it therefore does not indicate whether he was a bishop or only arrogated to himself the powers of a bishop. Whether, in fact, we have to do with monarchical authority at all depends on whether *ek tes ekklesias ekballei* does refer to excommunication. That *ekballo* ("to put out") is a technical term for banning someone from the synagogue or the church is often affirmed with an appeal to John 9:34f. for support.[53] But neither in that passage nor here does it clearly describe official action.[54] Yet *ekballei* in v. 10 is not to be taken as a rhetorical overstatement merely implying that Diotrephes was threatening to throw people out of the church.[55] Diotrephes

51. Thus Harnack, "Ueber der dritten Johannesbrief," followed by Käsemann, "Ketzer und Zeuge"; Günther Bornkamm, *Theological Dictionary of the New Testament*, VI, 670f., s.v. "*presbus*"; Bultmann, *Johannine Epistles*, 101 *n.* 12.

52. Cf. Arndt and Gingrich, "*epidechomai*." The positions taken by commentators on its meaning here are informed by their understanding of the situation and cannot be based simply on the meaning of the term.

53. Thus Käsemann, "Ketzer und Zeuge"; Bultmann, *Johannine Epistles*.

54. De Jonge, *De Brieven van Johannes*, 264; Schnackenburg, *Die Johannesbriefe*, 329; and W. Michaelis, *Einleitung in das Neue Testament* (Bern, 1961), 299, correctly view this as an unofficial action.

55. Such an explanation, advanced, for example, by Haenchen, "Neuere Literatur," 283f., would eliminate the problem that Gaius, had he been a member of Diotrephes' church, would have had to be excommunicated, but that we have no indication in the letter of such an action. On that understanding he would be running a serious risk when he receives the brethren,

does forbid members of the church to receive the emissaries, and he does eject them from the church when they persist. He is obviously in a position to do so, but it is not necessary to make him a monarchical bishop to explain his actions. Nor is it necessary to suppose that he asked the church for coercive measures against those of their number who acted against his wishes.[56] The picture that we get is of one man exercising his power, not of someone lobbying in order to impose his will.

The situation reflected is one in which power rather than ecclesiastical authority is exercised. The subject with which III John deals is hospitality, and the Elder accuses Diotrephes of refusing hospitality to strangers. It seems reasonable that *ekballo* should be understood as the opposite of *(hupo)lambano* and *epidechomai*, that is, that Diotrephes refused to extend hospitality any longer to those Christians who would oppose him in the matter. *Ekballei* suggests that they had been beneficiaries of his hospitality as members of the church that met in his house.[57] On such an understanding, *ek tes ekklesias ekballei* would have the same effect as the command given in II John 10—"do not receive (*lambanete*) him into the house" —the exclusion from the assembly meeting in a home, except that the latter is directed against the travelers, while in the former the action is extended to those who are already members of the local assembly. We have found no evidence that to have

---

and that would be the Elder's reason for praising him so much. Schnacken-burg, *Die Johannesbriefe*, 328, also considering Gaius to be one of those who wished to receive the brethren, claims that Gaius's hospitality is proof that Diotrephes did not actually have jurisdictional authority. However, the letter does not contain any evidence of a clash between Diotrephes and Gaius, and it is more reasonable to assume that Gaius was not subject to Diotrephes' actions.

56. Suggested by Dodd, *Johannine Epistles*, 162f.; Goguel, *Primitive Church*, 243f.

57. This was already suggested as a possibility by K. Braune, *The Epistles General of John*, in J. P. Lange, *A Commentary on the Holy Scriptures: Critical, Doctrinal and Homiletical* (New York, 1869), XXIV, 198.

a church meet in one's home bestowed any authority on the host. There is no indication that Gaius had any authority by virtue of his hospitality, and there is no need to assume it for Diotrephes. He may not have had ecclesiastical authority, but he did have the power to exclude from the assembly in his house those who opposed him. Whereas in *Didache* 11 we learn of traveling Christians abusing hospitality, in III John we have seen an individual who was extending it and using it for his own purpose.

ADDENDUM

Raymond Brown, in his recent commentary on the Johannine Epistles, is in general agreement with the view I have presented, but raises some objections to it:[58] 1. He does not understand v. 9 "to mean that Gaius knows the previous letter sent by the Presbyter or its contents. Indeed, the fact that the Presbyter has to tell Gaius that previously he wrote 'something to the church' of Diotrephes is an argument supporting the thesis that the two men do not belong to the same congregation"; 2. More importantly, he doubts that *ekklesia* in v. 9 refers to the church in the area, constituted of several local churches, but thinks that it means a local church as it does in v. 6; 3. He reads the letter as reflecting the Presbyter's attitude that Diotrephes and Gaius are not on an equal level; for instance, the Presbyter had earlier written to (the church of) Diotrephes but seemingly not to Gaius. As a possible variation of my view, Brown proposes that Gaius was neither a member of Diotrephes' house church nor fully the host, or head, of another house church, but rather a wealthy Christian in the area who had on several occasions extended hospitality to the "brothers" who had come from the Presbyter and been re-

58. Raymond E. Brown, *The Epistles of John.* Anchor Bible (New York, 1982), 730–32, 738.

fused by Diotrephes. The letter therefore not only requests Gaius to continue his hospitality, but may implicitly be suggesting that he "set up his house as a church meeting place."

The force of the first objection is weakened if my argument, that both the letter referred to in v. 9 and the one in III John are letters of recommendation, and that the former is called to mind in vv. 5–8, has any merit. If this was the case, there would be no need to rehearse the contents of the earlier letter. The Presbyter mentions the letter, not because Gaius does not know it, but does so for the sake of emphasis, as Brown's translation, "I did write something to the church," nicely brings out. The issue in this correspondence was hospitality. Having complimented Gaius for acceding to his request for support of the traveling brethren, he now turns to denounce Diotrephes for having rejected the letter and thereby also its writer.

The second objection correctly identifies what I consider the major weakness in my argument. It is true, as Brown indicates, that in Romans 16:4–5; I Corinthians 16:19, and Colossians 4:16, "church" is used for individual house churches, and my interpretation requires that I attribute two different meanings to it in the same context. It should be noted, however, that in the passages that Brown cites the churches are explicitly specified as being related to certain persons' houses, which is not the case here. Furthermore, I attach importance to what appears to have been the practice of writing one letter to a number of house churches in one area. I think it permits us to give a wider reference to "church" in v. 9 than just the group associated with Diotrephes. The third objection discovers a "difference of level" between Gaius and Diotrephes which escapes me, particularly since, on my reading, it is Gaius who receives two letters from the Presbyter.

As to Brown's suggestion with regard to Gaius, it is unclear to me of which church he is a member at the time III John is

written. I suspect Brown and I may differ on what we understand a house church to have been. To me the arrangement
seems to have been quite informal. In addition to the traveling
brethren (v. 5), there are *philoi* ("friends") with Gaius (v.
15). Brown regards the latter as friends of the Presbyter and
apparently does not think that they, together with Gaius, constitute a church. It appears more likely to me that "friends"
designate Christians associated with Gaius, and that the group
constituted a church.

In any case, Brown and I both realize that we are dealing,
at most, with probabilities when we interpret the details. His
commentary, certainly the most extensive one on the letter, is
noteworthy, among other things, for its focus on the social
dimension of the situation with which the letter deals, and in
that respect reflects the interest with which this book is
concerned.

Epilogue

For Intro
& paper

I WELCOME this opportunity to correct some typographical errors in the first edition[1] and to provide more recent bibliographical information on the works cited.[2] Interest in the social dimension of early Christianity has increased to such an extent that it is impossible in this brief epilogue to provide a survey of work that has been done during the seven years since the lectures on which the book is based were delivered. Such surveys of the literature and reflections on the enterprise

1. 26 *n.* 61, for A. R. Neumann read Horst Steckel; 30 *n.* 3, for *Studia Evangelica,* IV read *Studia Evangelica,* VI; p. 71 *n.* 25, for "and Paulus" read "und Paulus"; 91 *n.* 71, for 9148 read VI, 9148.
2. The following dissertations have now been published: Ronald F. Hock (4 *n.* 7; 24 *n.* 5), in revised form, *The Social Context of Paul's Ministry: Tentmaking and Apostleship* (Philadelphia, 1980); David L. Balch (4 *n.* 7; 50 *n.* 57), *Let Wives Be Submissive: The Domestic Code in 1 Peter* (Chico, Calif., 1981); Harry Y. Gamble (65 *n.* 13), *The Textual History of the Letter to the Romans* (Grand Rapids, Mich., 1977). E. A. Judge, "The Early Christians as a Scholastic Community" (45 *n.* 42) has been published, with notes partly updating the discussion, as "Die frühen Christen als scholastische Gemeinschaft," in Wayne A. Meeks (ed.), *Zur Soziologie des Urchristentums* (Munich, 1979), 131–64, and Chapter 2 of this volume appeared in the same book as "Soziale Ebene und literarische Bildung" (194–221). My article, "Hellenistic Moralists and the

113

are readily available and demonstrate that the investigation is proceeding in many directions.[3]

Attention can here be drawn to only a few major publications which can be expected to have considerable influence or to evoke reaction in future discussion. The publication, in German and English, of Gerd Theissen's important essays is sure to widen the circle of persons interested in the social description of early Christianity.[4] A collection of essays, largely by North American scholars, edited by Wayne Meeks and published in German, is likely to have the same effect,[5] as will

New Testament" (24 *n*. 54; 48 *n*. 50; 50 *n*. 57; 58 *n*. 59) has still not appeared; it is now scheduled for *Aufstieg und Niedergang der römischen Welt*, Part II, Vol. 26. The series in which my *Ancient Epistolary Theorists* (59 *n*. 82) was to be published did not materialize, and the essay was published in *Ohio Journal of Religious Studies*, V(1977), 3–77. My article, "The Inhospitality of Diotrephes" (70 *n*. 22) is printed as Chapter 4 of the present volume. Attention should also be drawn to Wayne A. Meeks and Robert L. Wilken, *Jews and Christians in Antioch in the First Four Centuries of the Common Era* (Missoula, Mont., 1978), which emerged from the American Academy of Religion/Society of Biblical Literature Working Group on the Social World of Early Christianity (3 *n*. 4), and to Dennis E. Smith, "Social Obligation in the Context of Communal Meals: A Study of the Christian Meal in 1 Corinthians in Comparison with Graeco-Roman Communal Meals" (Th.D. Dissertation, Harvard Divinity School, 1980), which reflects the interests of the Harvard group (p. 2).

3. See Robin Scroggs, "The Sociological Interpretation of the New Testament: The Present State of Research," *New Testament Studies*, XXVI (1980), 164–79, E. A. Judge, "The Social Identity of the First Christians: A Question of Method in Religious History," *Journal of Religious History*, XI(1980), 201–17; John H. Elliott, *A Home for the Homeless: A Sociological Exegesis of I Peter—Its Situation and Strategy* (Philadelphia, 1981), 1–20; John G. Gager, "Shall We Marry Our Enemies?: Sociology and the New Testament," *Interpretation*, XXXVII(1982), 256–65; Wayne A. Meeks, *The First Urban Christians: The Social World of the Apostle Paul* (New Haven, Conn., 1983), 1–8, who responds to criticisms of the enterprise.

4. Gerd Theissen, *Studien zur Soziologie des Urchristentums* (Tübingen, Germany, 1979); five of these studies appear in *The Social Setting of Pauline Christianity*, ed. and trans. with an introduction by John H. Schütz (Philadelphia, 1982). See also his *Sociology of Early Palestinian Christianity* (Philadelphia, 1978).

5. Meeks, *Zur Soziologie des Urchristentums*.

a collection by Robert Grant on a period later than the one considered here.[6] Howard Kee, in a broadly conceived book which he considers a trial run, and which ventures into the fields of anthropology, sociology of knowledge, and sociology of literature, sets forth methodological resources from the social sciences which may provide fresh paradigms for the study of early Christian literature.[7] On particular topics, William Countryman has written on wealth in the early church,[8] and Wolf-Henning Ollrog has studied Paul's co-workers.[9] John Schütz and Bengt Holmberg have demonstrated the results to be obtained by applying modern social theory to Paul's relationship with his churches.[10] John Elliott in a major volume has applied a method he describes as sociological exegesis to I Peter,[11] and Wayne Meeks, in a volume marked by respect for detail and its suggestive use of social theory, has undertaken to examine Paul from a sociological perspective.[12]

Some of the topics that I suggested might repay investigation have been taken up, not necessarily in response to my identification of them as worth pursuit. The popular philosophers have received some attention, witnessed by the publication of texts and translations of their works by the Society of Biblical Literature as well as studies devoted to particular subjects.[13]

6. Robert M. Grant, *Early Christianity and Society* (New York, 1977).
7. Howard Clark Kee, *Christian Origins in Sociological Perspective* (Philadelphia, 1980).
8. L. William Countryman, *The Rich Christian in the Church of the Early Empire: Contradictions and Accommodations* (New York, 1980).
9. Wolf-Henning Ollrog, *Paulus und seine Mitarbeiter* (Neukirchen-Vluyn, Germany, 1979).
10. John H. Schütz, *Paul and the Anatomy of Apostolic Authority* (Cambridge, 1975); Bengt Holmberg, *Paul and Power: The Structure of Authority in the Primitive Church as Reflected in the Pauline Epistles* (Philadelphia, 1980).
11. Elliott, *A Home for the Homeless.*
12. Meeks, *The First Urban Christians.*
13. Edward N. O'Neill (ed.), *Teles (The Cynic Teacher)* (Missoula, Mont., 1977); Abraham J. Malherbe (ed.), *The Cynic Epistles* (Missoula,

Among the latter, matters of literary interest have especially occupied investigators. The *Haustafeln* continue to attract interest, but now for their relevance in the attempt to situate early Christians in their society.[14] The question of the diatribe has again been taken up by Stanley Stowers, who claims that Paul's use of it does not reflect street-corner preaching, as has generally been held, but a school setting.[15] Benjamin Fiore has devoted a focused study to one feature of epistolary parae-

---

Mont., 1977); John Fitzgerald and L. Michael White, *The Tabula of Cebes* (Chico, Calif., 1983). I have attempted to sketch some of the differences between Stoicism and Cynicism in "Pseudo-Heraclitus, Epistle 4: The Divinization of the Wise Man," *Jahrbuch für Antike und Christentum*, XXI(1978), 42–64, and the diversity among Cynics in "Self-Definition among Cynics and Epicureans," in Ben F. Meyer and E. P. Sanders (eds.), *Jewish and Christian Self-Definition. Volume 3: Self-Definition in the Greco-Roman World* (Philadelphia, 1983), 46–59. Paul's appropriation and adaptation of popular philosophical traditions are treated by the present author in "Exhortation in First Thessalonians," *Novum Testamentum*, XXV(1983). The relevance of this material to the Pastoral Epistles is demonstrated in my "Medical Imagery in the Pastoral Epistles," W. Eugene March (ed.), *Texts and Testaments: Critical Essays in Honor of Stuart D. Currie* (San Antonio, 1980), 19–35. It is primarily David Balch who has demonstrated the importance of the Aristotelian and Pythagorean sources. See his *Let Wives Be Submissive* (n. 2); *idem*, "Household Ethical Codes in Peripatetic, Neopythagorean and Early Christian Moralists," *SBL 1977 Seminar Papers* (Missoula, Mont., 1977), 397–404; *idem*, "The Neopythagorean Moralists and the New Testament," H. Temporini and Wolfgang Haase (eds.), *Aufstieg und Niedergang der römischen Welt*, Vol. XXVI, Pt. II (forthcoming). Dieter Lührmann, "Wo man nicht Sklave oder Freier is. Überlegungen zur Struktur frühchristlicher Gemeinden," in *Wort und Dienst, Jahrbuch der theologischen Schule Bethel*, XIII(1973), 53–83, had independently arrived at the Aristotelian sources; cf. also his "Neutestamentliche Haustafeln und antike Ökonomie," *New Testament Studies*, XXVII(1980), 83–97.

14. See Balch and Lührmann (n. 13), Elliott (n. 3), and cf. Klaus Thraede, "Zum historischen Hintergrund der 'Haustafeln' des NT," in Ernst Dassmann and K. Suso Frank, *Pietas. Festschrift für Bernhard Kötting. Jahrbuch für Antike und Christentum Ergänzungsband*, VIII (1980), 359–68.

15. Stanley Kent Stowers, *The Diatribe and Paul's Letter to the Romans* (Chico, Calif., 1981); *idem.*, "Social Status, Public Speaking and Private Teaching: The Circumstances of Paul's Preaching Activity," *Novum Testamentum*, XXV(1983).

nesis.[16] In addition, a beginning has been made to make the area of popular philosophical ethics more accessible to New Testament scholars.[17] It is true to say, however, that this specialized area of study has not been overrun by eager investigators. Much more awaits attention, not only with respect to the Stoics and Cynics, who have traditionally received most attention, but also the Pythagoreans and Epicureans. Until the philosophers' works are known and their relevance to the New Testament is convincingly demonstrated, we may continue to expect the puzzlement and skepticism which these first attempts on occasion meet.[18]

Materials other than the philosophical are increasingly brought into the discussion. For example, rhetorical theory and practice have been used, preeminently by Hans Dieter Betz, to cast light on the New Testament.[19] But there are vast areas that have hardly been touched. I wish to mention again the satirists. Studies like that by J. Gérard on Juvenal demonstrate how a sensitivity for Roman society can be developed by careful reading of these social critics.[20] East Europeans, sometimes heavy-handedly and tiresomely, tend to read the literature in this way, and we can well afford to do so likewise, but with greater care.[21]

16. Benjamin Fiore, S.J., "The Function of Personal Example in the Socratic and Pastoral Epistles" (Ph.D. Dissertation, Yale University, 1982).
17. Hans Dieter Betz (ed.), *The Ethical Writings of Plutarch and Early Christian Literature* (Leiden, Holland, 1978).
18. As reflected, for example, in the reviews by A. E. Harvey of my *Cynic Epistles* in *Journal of Theological Studies*, New Series XXX(1979), 312–14, and G. A. Muddiman of the first edition of this book, *ibid.*, XXXII (1981), 252–53.
19. Hans Dieter Betz, *Galatians: A Commentary on Paul's Letter to the Churches in Galatia*. Hermeneia—A Critical and Historical Commentary on the Bible (Philadelphia, 1979).
20. J. Gérard, *Juvénal et la réalité contemporaine* (Paris, 1976).
21. The conference proceedings referred to on p. 58 *n.* 78 are a good example. The articles in Johannes Irmscher and Kurt Treu (eds.), *Das Korpus Griechischen Christlicher Schriftsteller: Historie, Gegenwart,*

The issue of the social level of early Christians continues to elicit interest.[22] Robin Scroggs has raised some trenchant questions about what I suggested might be a new emerging consensus, and he has received a response from E. A. Judge.[23] Wayne Meeks has now treated the subject with greater sophistication and in a manner that promises to be more fruitful for the study of early Christian communities than merely pegging some of their number on the social scale.[24] The discussion has therefore moved well beyond what I attempted, but I feel obligated to clarify my position since it has been misconstrued.

I related my discussion of social status to what appeared to be a consensus. However, I limited myself in order to illustrate this generally held view by referring to Marxists and especially to Adolf Deissmann. Pointing to recent work on the subject, I suggested that a new consensus, if it was not premature to speak of one, might be emerging—one which differed from the consensus represented by Deissmann, who emphasized that Christians had come from the lower strata of society (p. 31). In supporting the emerging consensus which drew attention to the presence of persons from the higher social strata in Christian communities, I offered evidence from the literary level of some New Testament writings and introduced the work of Gerd Theissen. Perhaps, since I was concentrating on the writers, I was not expansive enough, but I certainly did not wish to leave the impression that there existed Christian

Zukunft, Vol. CXX of *Texte und Untersuchungen* (Berlin, 1977), discuss whether future editions of *Griechischen christlichen Schriftsteller der ersten drei Jahrhunderte* should not reflect contemporary social and economic interests.

22. See B. Grimm, *Untersuchungen zur sozialen Stellung der frühen Christen in der römischen Gesellschaft* (Dissertation, Bamberg, Germany, 1975); Ronald F. Hock, "Paul's Tentmaking and the Problem of His Social Class," *Journal of Biblical Literature*, XCVII(1978), 555–64; Stowers, "Social Status" (*n.* 15).

23. Scroggs, "The Sociological Interpretation" (*n.* 3), 169–71; Judge, "The Social Identity" (*n.* 3), 207–9.

24. Meeks, *The First Urban Christians* (*n.* 3), 51–75.

communities largely made up of people from the upper strata. I was explicit that the literary evidence was a complement to other data (p. 33). I called attention to the different levels of literary finesse of New Testament writers (p. 33) and cautioned that we should consider the possibility that Paul's rhetorical and literary ability differed from that of the people to whom he wrote (pp. 56f.). In presenting Theissen's views on the Corinthians, I questioned some of the criteria he used to classify certain persons as members of the upper strata, and similarly some of Judge's proposals.[25] Nevertheless, I agreed with Judge and Theissen that those individuals were a dominant minority in Corinth[26] and concluded that Theissen's sketch of the social stratification in the church marked a considerable advance (p. 86). Where I do differ most clearly from Theissen is in my higher estimate of the importance of theological as compared to sociological grounds on the conflicts in Corinth (84, cf. 78).

I am therefore surprised by the recent comments of John Gager. In a review of my book, he comments on my description of the new consensus and says:

In large part, the proponents of this new view see themselves as correcting earlier presentations of early Christianity as exclusively proletarian, a movement of slaves, laborers, and outcasts of various sorts. While it may be seriously doubted that such a view ever existed apart from a few romantics and early Marxists, this renewed interest in the issue of social location will undoubtedly contribute to a better understanding of these persistently controversial matters.[27]

I would have thought that he would agree with my description of the old consensus, for he had earlier also written of it:

25. On Theissen, see pp. 73 *n.* 27, 75, 76, 80 *n.* 41; on Judge, pp. 45, 56.

26. See pp. 29f., 72. For Theissen's own statements, see *The Social Setting of Pauline Christianity*, 72ff.

27. John G. Gager, in *Religious Studies Review*, V(1979), 179.

It is only in recent years, and primarily among such classicists as A. D. Nock, A. H. M. Jones, and E. R. Dodds, that the social constituency of early Christianity has again come into focus. Among this limited circle, something approaching a consensus has emerged on two aspects of the social question: first, that for more than two hundred years Christianity was essentially a movement among disprivileged groups in the Empire; and second, that its appeal among these groups depended on social as much as ideological considerations.[28]

It would appear to me that the effect of this statement on the consensus, which Gager evidently accepted, is to widen the consensus beyond the few romantics and early Marxists whom I had mentioned. Gager has now either shifted ground somewhat, as Judge suggests,[29] or his qualifications in the two statements ("in large part," "exclusively," "essentially") obscure what he really means.

Equally surprising is Gager's classification of my view in relation to Theissen's. In a recent article, commenting on the debate about the social status of early Christians, he writes:

One side of the debate, represented by Theissen and myself, holds that most of the members of Christian communities came from the lower classes. The other side, represented by E. A. Judge, Abraham Malherbe, Robert Grant, holds that "the triumph of Christianity took place from the top down." Some of the disagreements between the two parties are quite insubstantial. No one, for instance, denies that *some* believers were educated and stood relatively high in the social hierarchy of their local towns and cities. But what ought to concern us is not the few but the majority and thus the character of the movement as a whole.[30]

The quotation, which is inadvertently attributed in a footnote to page 11 of my book, is actually a partial quotation from page 11 of Grant's *Early Christianity and Society,* where Grant

28. John G. Gager, *Kingdom and Community: The Social World of Early Christianity* (Englewood Cliffs, N.J., 1975), 96. I refer to this page on p. 31 *n.* 6 and identify Gager with the old consensus.

29. Judge, "The Social Identity," 207 *n.* 18.

30. Gager, "Shall We Marry Our Enemies?" 262.

120

states the case for the importance of Constantine's conversion for the Christianization of the Roman world. In this context, the full statement reads: "The triumph of Christianity in a hierarchically organized society necessarily took place from the top down." My interest lies in the first century and in relationships within the church. More to the point is that the way in which the two positions are presented may lead to the inference that I do not think that the majority of Christians were from the lower strata. Certainly that was the case in Corinth, but as Theissen has demonstrated so well, there the minority dominated the situation. And how we can hope to gain a firmer grasp on the character of the movement as a whole by not being concerned with those persons from the relatively higher social strata who wrote the documents which constitute our primary access to the communities, and who figured importantly in the communities themselves, as Theissen has shown, escapes me.

When I first wrote, not much had been written about house churches. That is no longer the case. The subject is now finding its way into commentaries, for example that of Raymond Brown (cf. Chapter 4) and Joachim Gnilka's on Philemon.[31] Robert Banks has also offered an interpretation of Paul's thought from the perspective of house churches as the setting of Christian life.[32] Also, the household theme, if not precisely the house church, has been examined by Elliott in his study of I Peter.[33] Hans-Josef Klauck has written a short book, primarily historical in orientation, on the subject.[34] Most recently

31. Joachim Gnilka, *Der Philemonbrief* (Freiburg, Germany, 1982), 17–33.
32. Robert Banks, *Paul's Idea of Community: The Early House Churches in their Historical Setting* (Grand Rapids, Mich., 1980).
33. Elliott, *A Home for the Homeless,* esp. Chap. 4.
34. Hans-Josef Klauck, *Hausgemeinde und Hauskirche im frühen Christentum* (Stuttgart, Germany, 1981). See also his summary of the book, "Die Hausgemeinde als Lebensform im Urchristentum," *Münchener Theologischen Zeitschrift,* XXXII(1981), 1–15.

Michael White has provided us with the most extensive collection of evidence for the institution as well as an interpretation of the data.[35] One expects that the discussion will continue as the questions are posed more sharply and the method of treating them is refined.

I have been criticized quite properly for my indiscriminate use of "social" and "sociological."[36] I have difficulty accepting, however, the suggestion that "social description" be used for the type of investigation that I have attempted, and that "sociological" be reserved for analysis or interpretation that makes use of the methods and models of the discipline of sociology. Such a limitation of the latter seems to me to be arbitrary. In any case, the time is rapidly approaching when we should take stock of what has been accomplished in this area of investigation. What is needed is an accurate, extensive, and systematic presentation and assessment of the results that have been obtained so far, as well as a judicious analysis and evaluation of the various approaches to the material that have been made under the umbrella of sociology. Such an essay would contribute immeasurably to the enterprise that will indeed occupy scholars of Christian antiquity for some time to come.

35. Lloyd Michael White, "Domus Ecclesiae: Domus Dei" (Ph.D. Dissertation, Yale University, 1982).

36. By Gager in *Religious Studies Review*, V(1979), 179, cf. 175. On the issue, see also Elliott, *A Home for the Homeless*, 3.

Index

Acts of the Apostles: 5:39, p. 42; 9:2, p. 102n; 11:1ff., p. 66; 14:23, pp. 70, 101n; 15:3, p. 96n; 16:14, p. 95n; 16:15, 31ff., p. 97n; 17: 5–9, p. 97; 17:6f., pp. 96n, 97n; 17:28, p. 43; 18:1–3, p. 95n; 18: 1–8, p. 97n; 18:3, p. 90; 18:8, pp. 72, 73; 18:10, p. 73; 18:18ff., p. 90; 18:27, pp. 96n, 102n; 19:9, p. 89; 19:11, 12, p. 90; 19:23, p. 91; 20:17, pp. 70, 101n; 20:31–35, p. 90; 20:38, p. 96n; 21:4ff., 7f., 15f., pp. 68, 96n; 21:17, p. 96n; 22:3, p. 34; 22:5, p. 102n; 26:14, p. 42; 28:2, p. 96n; 28:7, p. 96n; 28:10, p. 96n

Afanasieff, N., 61n, 101n
Albright, William F., 14n
Allen, Roland, 62
Almqvist, H., 99n
Analogy, in historical study, 14n, 48, 60, 87
Anastos, Milton V., 21n
Anthologies, 42, 43
Apollonius of Tyana, 46n

Apologies, literary character of, 16, 22, 23
Aquila and Priscilla, 64, 74, 74n, 75, 90, 95n
Aratus, 43
Archaeological data, 2, 15, 30, 75
Aristotelian sources, 116n
Arndt, William F., 106n, 108n
Artisans, 31, 75, 77. See also Labor, manual
Associations: meals of, 79, 82; membership of, 78, 87; and the church, 87–88
Athenagoras, 90n

Balch, David L., 4n, 50n, 113n, 116n
Banks, Robert, 121
Banquets, influenced Christian worship, 79–84 passim
Barbour, Hugh, 38n
Bardtke, Hans, 88n
Bartchy, S. Scott, 4n, 85n
Bartelink, G. J. M., 40n
Bauer, Walter, 93, 93n

123

Index

Criticism: of Christians, 22–22; of Epicureans, 25–26
Crouch, James E., 50n, 51n
Cullmann, Oscar, 96n
Cults: and the schools, 54n; meals of, 79, 79n; membership of, 84, 85; social constitution of, 78, 87. *See also* Isis, cult of
Currie, Stuart D., 116n
Cynics: dictum of, 90n, 117; letters of, 13, 14; opinions about, 49; organization of, 14; propaganda of, 13, 19

Dahl, Nils A., 59n, 70n, 92n
Danielou, Jean, 16n
Danker, Frederick W., 42n
Dassmann, Ernst, 116n
Deissmann, Adolf: social interpretation of, 31–59 *passim*, 118; on genealogical and analogical parallels, 14n; on Kautsky, 31–32; on letters and epistles, 57–59; on New Testament language, 35–41 *passim*; on papyri, 19n, 32–33
Demetrius, 105–6
Demonax, 49
Diatribe: quotations in, 42; related to social context, 50, 116; and the New Testament, 39
Dibelius, Martin, 31n
Didache, 96n, 101n
Diet, 79–81
Dihle, Albrecht, 42n, 49
Dill, Samuel, 14n
Dio Chrysostom, 19–20, 44, 45, 46n, 49, 50n, 77n, 95n
Diotrephes, 70n, 92–112
Dobschütz, Ernst von, 10, 13n
Dodd, C. H., 103n *passim*
Dodds, E. R., 120
Dombrowski, B. W., 88n

Donfried, Karl P., 27n, 50n
Doty, William G., 57n

Economic conditions of Christians, 8–9
Education, 8, 34, 40–45 *passim*, 55, 56, 59
Ehrhardt, Arnold, 79n
Elliott, John H., 114n, 115 *passim*
Ellis, Earle E., 64n; 95n
Eltester, Walther, 5n, 21n
Emeljanow, Victor, 14n
Ephesus: church in, 74, 89–91; guilds in, 89; Paul in, 64
Epictetus, 46n, 50n
Epicureans: criticism of, 22, 25–26, 117; and Christians, 25–28
Epimenides, 43
Erastus, 72, 74, 80
Ethics, 46, 48, 49
Euripides, 42, 43, 44
Eusebius, 52n
Exhortation. *See Haustafel*, Paraenesis

Farmer, William R., 16n
Faye, G. La, 63n
Festugiére, A. J., 25n
Filson, Floyd, 61n, 96n
Fiore, Benjamin, 117, 117n
Fitzgerald, John T., 116n
Foerster, Werner, 5n
Frank, K. Suso, 116n
Friedrich, Gerhard, 35n
Fritz, Kurt von, 14n
Frohnes, Heinzgünter, 40n, 63n, 64n
Funk, Robert W., 16n, 103n

Gagé, J., 85n
Gager, John G., 3n, 10n, 11n, 12n,

125

Index

53; 4:8–10, pp.67, 115; Second
Letter of, 2:21, p.41
Philemon, Letter to: 68, 96n, 97n,
100n, 101n, 102n
Philemon, Letter to, 68, 96n, 97n,
96n, 102n, 103n; 4:2–3, p.102n
Philo, 51, 52, 54, 63n
Philodemus, 24–25
Philosophers: as reformers, 23, 44;
study of, 115–17; use of proverbs
by, 44. See also Cynics, Epicureans, Pythagoreans, Stoics
Phoebe, 98, 98n
Plümacher, Eckhard, 30n, 44n, 90n
Plutarch, 25n, 82, 117n
Polycarp, 96n
Preachers, mobility of, 64
Preaching: importance of, 11, 12,
77; and house churches, 69–70
Preisker, Herbert, 7
Prisca, 95n
Proletariat, 8–9, 30–31
Proselytes, 30n, 51–53, 64, 67
Prosopography, 47
Proverbs, 41–44
Pseudo-Plato, 103n
Pythagoreans: communities of, 14;
literature of, 14, 15, 116n, 117

Quotations, classical: Aratus, 43;
Epimenides, 43; Euripides, 42;
Menander, 42; proverbs, 41–42

Rabbow, Paul, 54n
Radke, G., 63n
Ramsay, William, 63n, 95n
Reicke, Bo, 98n, 99n
Reitzenstein, Richard, 19n
Renan, Ernest, 91n
Renehan, Robert, 41n
Revolutionary movement, Christianity as, 9, 31

Rhetoric: instruction in, 44, 55–56;
and letter-writing, 57–59; Paul's,
46, 54–59; theory of, 117. See
also Sophist
Riddle, Donald W., 16n, 95n
Rigaux, Beda, 57n
Robinson, James M., 1n, 12n
Romans, Letter to the: 12:8, p.98;
12:13, p.96n; 13:9–13, p.67;
15:23f., pp.68, 96n; 16, pp.64–
65, 95n, 100, 101n; 16:2, pp.
96n, 98, 102n, 103n; 16:3ff., p.
97n; 16:5, 14, 15, pp.70, 100;
16:23, pp.73, 97
Rordorff, Willy, 61n
Rosén, H. B., 42n
Rostovtzeff, Michael, 5
Rusche, Helga, 66n, 95n
Rydbeck, Lars, 40–41

Sanday, W., 98n
Sanders, E. P., 116n
Satirists, 20, 117
Schatkin, Margaret, 41n
Schille, Gottfried, 64n
Schmidt, Peter, 30n
Schnackenburg, R., 103n passim
Schneider, Carl, 5n
Schneider, Norbert, 55n
Scholarship, American biblical, and
the social sciences, 2–6
Schools: philosophical, 8, 48–54;
and the cults, 54n; secondary, 43,
44, 55–56
Schrage, Wolfgang, 50n
Schreiner, K., 31n
Schubert, H. von, 90n
Schumacher, Rudolf, 4n, 31n
Schütz, John H., 114n, 115, 115n
Scroggs, Robin, 59n, 114n, 118,
118n
Seneca, 48n, 58

129